Landscape Design

Theory and Practice

M. PRATAP RAO
Architect-Planner
B.Arch, MURP, AIIA, AITP, AIID

STANDARD PUBLISHERS DISTRIBUTORS
1705-B, NAI SARAK, POST BOX No.: 1066, DELHI-110006
Phone: 01123262700, 01123285798, Fax: 011-23243180
Show Room: 4581/15 G.F., ANSARI ROAD, DARYAGANJ, NEW DELHI-110002
www.standardpublishers.com www.engineeringbooks.co.in email: stpub@vsnl.com

Published by:
A.K. Jain
For Standard Publishers Distributors
1705-B, Nai Sarak, Delhi-110006.

Show Room:
4581/15 G.F., Ansari Road,
Daryaganj, New Delhi-110002.
Phone: 011-23281159

First Edition: 2011

Price: Rs. 200.00

ISBN: 978-81-8014-184-3

Laser Typesetting by: Ajesh Bhargave, Delhi.
Printed by: Prabhat Offset Press, Delhi.

PREFACE

Landscape design is a fast developing profession with increasing awareness about the need to protect the environment. Building is not just constructing the physical structure. Landscape design is also important for the building to be a pleasant place. In landscaping, there are a lot of outdoor elements to consider. These elements are not only aesthetic in nature but functional also. The climate, the position of the building relative to the sun, the types of plants and trees, ground cover and paving, water and placement of electrical and water lines is very important. There is also the landscaping budget to consider for maintenance. Careful planning is crucial to landscape design.

There is even greater need of planned landscape for factories and industries. Most factories are nothing more than the glorified sheds. It is landscaping which can provide aesthetically satisfactory solutions by providing beautiful parks, playgrounds, attractive location of services, stores and network of roads planted with flowering trees. Factories and industries planned in this manner have shown improved morale and cheerfulness among the workers.

One may ask, whether landscaping is possible in present days of land shortages and high-rise buildings? No doubt, it is possible to create a beautiful landscape even around small buildings within the limits of available space. In case of high-rise buildings, the open terrace of each apartment can be utilised on the lines of Hanging Gardens at Babylon. These types of terrace gardens are becoming much more popular in high-rise buildings of metropolitan cities. With the coming of industrial revolution, the horrifying effects of population explosion and sudden growth of concrete jungles with abuse and disregard to nature started.

The main purpose of landscaping is to create a healthy environment and give the occupants a healthy breath, good appearance and natural beauty. In ancient times the landscape design was merely gardening, but it has gradually evolved. Two main components of the environment have to be considered; the man-made component, which involves man's intervention like the construction of roads, bridges, buildings along with all the necessary infrastructure; and the natural environment like space, water, trees, rocks and the earth. As such the landscape design has to consider not the inner spaces alone but to harmonize inner spaces with those outside. Landscape design is not limited to design of gardens and parks but it takes into account the entire area of the city and countryside, characteristics of physical features, topography etc. Unfortunately, the concept of ecosystem was lost. Good environment is essential for the well-being of the people.

This book covers the syllabus on 'Landscape Design' of both degree and diploma courses. This book is divided into 12 chapters as shown below:

1. Introduction
2. History of landscape design
3. Basics of Landscape Design
4. Site Planning
5. Planting design
6. Garden design
7. Garden styles
8. Plant management
9. Hard & Soft landscape
10. Landscape Construction
11. Landscape Design Code
12. Landscape design terminology

There are model questions at the end of each chapter. I would appreciate and welcome all suggestions from the readers to improve the content of the book in future editions.

— M. PRATAP RAO

CONTENTS

1 Introduction

Landscaping refers to any activity that modifies the visible features of an area of land. It includes living flora and fauna, natural elements, terrain shape, water bodies and other habitations.

People want two things from the natural environment: utility and beauty. All material progress in civilization has consisted in the modification of the surroundings to serve these two needs. The role of landscape design is to guide modification of the landscape to get maximum aesthetic satisfaction while meeting both these needs. It could be formal surroundings of a palace or a place of rest. The landscape architect or designer must have knowledge of nature, natural materials and sensitivity to the natural beauty of rock, wood and water.

There has been a general recognition of the value of designed and organized cities, parks and other out door spaces. There is also increased interest in private pleasure grounds of various kinds. There is now an effective demand for designing skill using as materials ground forms and vegetation. Designing skill is required in the arrangement of landscape and architectural forms like streets, parks and buildings for public use.

The landscape designer should know the materials of his art: ground forms, vegetation and structures in their relation to landscape. The landscape designer cannot produce at will all the forms but choose from among the forms offered by nature those which will suit the purpose. A good design is possible of execution with accurate first-hand knowledge of the plant materials and the ground forms for composition. Beauty of vegetation lies in intricacy, multiplicity, growth and change. The fundamental organization of natural designs preserves and enhances natural scenery. The landscape designer must study the forces, which carve the valleys and direct the flow of the streams. Keen interest to know the aesthetic unity of a mountain or the perfect growth of a ground-covering fern is necessary to decorate nature-inspired work.

It is necessary to know the distinction among the following nomenclature normally used in landscape design to avoid ambiguity for better understanding.

1. **Landscape design** is an independent profession and a design and art tradition, practiced by Landscape designers, combining nature and culture. In contemporary practice Landscape design bridges between landscape architecture and garden design.

2. **Landscape architecture** is the design of outdoor and public spaces to achieve environmental, socio-behavioral, and aesthetic effects. It involves the systematic investigation of existing social, ecological, and geological conditions in the landscape. A practitioner in the profession of landscape architecture is called a landscape architect. Landscape Architecture is an organized profession. Its members have approved qualifications and work on Garden Design, Landscape Design, Landscape Planning and other specialized activities. The relationship between Landscape Design and Landscape Architecture is equivalent to the relationship between the law and lawyers. The term landscape architecture was invented by Gilbert Laing Meason in 1828. 'Landscape architecture' is now recognized by the International Labour Organization and represented by the International Federation of Landscape Architects (IFLA). Most countries have professional associations concerned with landscape architecture.

   A landscape designer generally works only with plants and 'softscaping' theoretically designing or including structures such as walls and pathways. A designer can provide complex landscape plan. A landscape architect is more inclined to include very detailed information on the 'hardscaping' specifying details about the structure of a wall or paving. A landscape architect will provide a highly detailed landscape plan drawn to scale including specifications. A landscape engineer will add construction detail and specifications. All landscape architects are landscape designers but not all landscape designers are landscape architects. A Landscape Designer is an amateur, whereas a Landscape Architect is a professional.

3. **Horticulture** is the science of plant cultivation including the process of preparing soil for the planting of seeds, tubers, or cuttings. Horticulturists work and conduct research in the disciplines of plant propagation and cultivation, crop production, plant breeding and genetic engineering, plant biochemistry, and plant physiology. The work basically involves fruits, berries, nuts, vegetables, flowers, trees, shrubs, and turf. Horticulturists work to improve crop yield, quality, nutritional value, and resistance to insects, diseases, and environmental stresses. Horticulture usually refers to gardening on a smaller scale, while agriculture refers to the large-scale cultivation of crops. The word is composite, from two words, *horti*, meaning grass in the Greek and the word "culture".

A. Design Process

A landscape design process includes scrupulous analysis and design of the site, plant selection and development of design details.

1. Site analysis:

A complete site survey and analysis of existing conditions should be undertaken including an inventory of both natural and built features. Site factors of fundamental concern relative to both the retention of existing, as well as the installation of new, plant materials include:

1. Visual factors.
2. Climatic data.
3. Existing vegetation.
4. Soil.
5. Hydrology.
6. Topography/slope analysis.
7. Spatial analysis.

8. Program analysis.
9. Circulation patterns.
10. Noise factors.
11. Security requirements.
12. Maintenance requirements.

2. Programming:

Before a landscape design is begun, development of a program is necessary. The program consists of a description of user requirements and environmental design objectives. User needs, environmental problems and maintenance capabilities should be carefully and thoroughly studied. The extent of the planting will vary with each class and category of facility. The function and prominence of the facility should be the guiding factor in determining the scope of design.

3. Conceptual design:

After site analysis and program data, work on a conceptual design should begin. This involves arranging of plant material masses to satisfy the needs and requirements established by the site analysis and program. Plant masses should be arranged in terms of intended use and size rather than according to species or variety. The primary concern of the conceptual design phase is to provide solutions to the functional requirements of the site so that preliminary cost and phasing plans can be developed. The hardscape items like pavement, seating, steps and walls should be included.

4. Specification of plant materials:

After a satisfactory conceptual design is developed and adequate funding is assured, a final plan should be prepared. This involves interpreting the desired forms and sizes of plant masses into specific plant selections. A thorough knowledge of available plant materials and their characteristics is required.

5. Final landscape plan:

The final landscape plan consists of a series of working drawings and a set of specifications. These documents are used by the landscape contractor for bidding and constructing the project. Working drawings, with the exception of construction details, are based on a scale drawing of the site. The type and number of drawings required for a particular project may vary, but usually include the plans described below:

1. **Planting plan:** The planting plan shows the location and names of all plant materials. The following information about each plant species should be included on or with the plan:
   — Common and botanical names.
   — Size.
   — Type of root preparation (*i.e.*, container-grown, balled and bare-rooted).
   The required quantity of each plant should be indicated in the plant list.

2. **Staking and layout plan:** The locations of trees, shrubs, plant beds, hedges and other elements which pertain to planting are

illustrated on the staking and layout plan. The exact location of each element is determined by measuring distances from established baselines. In the case of very large sites, from coordinates of a grid system developed for the site.

3. **Landscape grading plan:** The landscape-grading plan includes information for finish grading of lawns, henna and shrub beds. This plan should be coordinated with other grading and drainage plans for the project.

4. **Irrigation plan:** An irrigation plan should include the location, size and type of sprinkler heads, drip emitters, pipelines, manual or automatic valves and the water source and meter. Symbols for the various components of the system should be included. Detail drawings which illustrate back-flow prevention devices, system construction and assembly requirements or installation of various components of the system may be added to the plan.

5. **Construction details:** Detail drawings are used to clarify the construction requirements of various components of a landscape project such as paved landscape areas, retaining walls, footbridges, benches and fences. Detail drawings should include sizes and dimensions of materials to be used and construction techniques. Cross sections and elevations may be used to convey this information.

6. **Specifications and cost estimation:** Specifications for the project include technical data to support information contained in the working drawings. Cost estimates may be used for establishing a budget and a phasing schedule for construction of the project.

EXERCISE

1. Explain the need and importance of Landscape Design.
2. Distinguish the nomenclature commonly used with reference to Landscape Design.
3. Explain the Landscape Design process normally adopted.

2

History of Landscape Design

The history of gardening extends at least 4000 years of human civilization. Egyptian tomb paintings of the 1500s BC are of the earliest physical evidence of decorative landscape design. They show lotus ponds surrounded by symmetrical rows of acacias and palms. Another ancient gardening tradition is of Persia. The Hanging Gardens of Babylon are renowned as one of the Wonders of the World. Persian gardens were normally organized symmetrically along a center line known as an axis. Persian influences extended to post-Alexander's Greece. Around 350 BC there were gardens at the Academy of Athens and Theophrastus. Epicurus also had a garden where he walked and taught, and gave it to *Hermarchus* of *Mytilene*. The most significant ancient gardens in the western world were the Ptolemy's gardens at *Alexandria*. The gardening tradition brought to Rome by *Lucullus*. Rich Romans built extensive villa gardens with water features, topiary and cultivated roses and shaded arcades.

Fig 2.1. Garden of versailles, France

Fig 2.2. Typical Wild garden

Fig 2.3. Academy of Athens, Greece

Byzantium and Moorish Spain kept garden traditions alive after the fall of Rome. Around this time a separate gardening tradition had arisen in China. This was carried to Japan, where it developed into aristocratic miniature landscapes centered on ponds. Then they developed into Zen gardens of temples.

In Europe, gardening revived in *Languedoc* and the *Ile-de-France* in the 13th century. The rediscovery of descriptions of antique Roman villas and gardens led to the creation of a new form of garden known as the Italian Renaissance garden in the late 15th and early

16th century. The formal *Garden à la française*, exemplified by the *Gardens of Versailles*, became the dominant style of garden in Europe until the middle of the 18th century. Then it was replaced by the English and the French landscape gardens. The 19th century saw a number of historical revivals and Romantic cottage-inspired gardening. In England, William Robinson and Gertrude Jekyll were strong proponents of the wild garden and the perennial garden respectively. Andrew Jackson Downing and Frederick Law Olmsted adapted European styles for North America influencing public parks, campuses and suburban landscapes. Olmsted's influence extended into the 20th century.

Fig 2.4. Hanging Gardens of Babylon, Iraq

Fig 2.5. Typical Perennial garden

Fig 2.6. Typical Zen Garden

The 20th century also saw the influence of modernism in the garden from Thomas Church's kidney-shaped swimming pool to the bold colors and forms of Roberto Burle-Marx. Strong environmental consciousness is driving new aspects in gardening today. The historical development of garden styles is briefly given below.

A. Persian gardens

All Persian gardens were developed to protect from the harsh and arid landscape of the Iranian Plateau. Historical European gardens were carved from their existing landscape. Persian gardens developed in strong contrast to the hostile environment. The heart of Persia (Present day Iran) was high and dry. A series of basins and plateaus are separated by the two main mountain ranges, the Albourz and the Zagros.

Since ancient times, lush gardens have grown in the region due to an ingenious engineering system of underground aqueducts called qanats. Originating in northeastern Persia around 800BC, qanats brought the water from the snow melt to the plains for irrigation and human use. The abundance of water became the essence of the Persian garden. A rich variety of species flourished. Thin channels delivered water throughout the garden. Water was feeding fountains, ponds, cooling the air and providing tender music.

Persian gardens were places for poetry, privacy and contemplation. They were not limited to pleasure and retreat. Gardens were central to the political life of the ruling class throughout Persian history. The Achaemenian king Cyrus placed his throne within his garden at Pasargadae. Persian miniature paintings from the 15th to the 17th century depict kings receiving diplomats in their gardens. Treaties were signed; feasts and celebrations took place in gardens. All important moments of national identity with depictions of legendary loves were shown in gardens.

The ancient gardens before Cyrus and his descendents show characteristics which define gardens in Persia. They also show places from India to Spain which drew on Persian ideas. Gardens were divided into quadrants by channels of water punctuated by geometrically shaped basins. At a central intersection point was a platform for viewing. It later evolved into a formal open pavilion decorated with coffered ceiling structures representing the complexity of the heavens. Geometry of the ordered universe was kept throughout Persian gardens. The surface design features basic ground plane and its fourfold *'chahar bagh'* format. It represents the four corners of the world and the four rivers of paradise predominately associated with the Islamic period.

Persian designs have a natural affinity to certain Islamic concepts. They were so deeply embedded in the culture maintaining their Persian character throughout the country's turbulent history. The relationship of architecture to the Persian garden is influenced by climate and geography. It was also infused with a sense of the passing qualities of light and reflection. The interior and exterior spaces were transparent with the use of carved screens, deep archways, multiple vaults and honeycomb patterned ceilings with tiny windows of light. Persian gardens can be viewed in relation to their classical tradition of painting during the *Safavid* period.

The Islamic gardens of Spain during the 14th century are far more elaborate than north European gardens of that period. The designs were influenced by the *Moors* featuring open garden rooms, intricate tile designs, water features and sculpture. These gardens had flowery outdoor spaces. Members of the court could meet and cool themselves from the severe heat of the sun. The Alhambra Palace and the Generalife gardens that surround the palace in Grenada, Spain survive till today showing the Moors mark on Spanish landscape design.

B. Egyptian gardens

Egyptian Gardens were maintained for secular purposes and attached to temple compounds. Gardens in private homes were used for growing vegetables and located near a canal or the river. They were often surrounded by walls. The gardens were used for pleasure and beauty besides utility. Gardens were used to produce foodstuff, flowers and for medicinal purposes. The poor used the gardens for growing vegetables. The rich people lined them with sheltering trees and decorative pools. Wooden structures formed pergolas to support vines of grapes to produce raisins and wine. The gardens also had elaborate ornamental stone kiosks with decorative statues.

Fig 2.7. Typical Egyptian gardens

Fig 2.8. Typical Hellenistic gardens

Fig 2.9. The Gardens of Lucullus, Rome, Italy

Temple gardens had plots for cultivating special vegetables, plants or herbs. They were used to perform temple rituals. Gardens were laid out according to temple principles. Avenues leading to the entrance of the temple were lined with trees. Central courtyards had small gardens. The space between temple buildings maintained gardens with trees, vineyards, flowers and ponds.

The ancient Egyptian garden was more like a collection of herbs or a patch of wild flowers without the specially bred flowers of today. Gardens needed constant attention and depended on irrigation due to the arid climate of Egypt. Skilled gardeners were employed by temples and wealthy households to maintain gardens.

C. Hellenistic gardens

The Egyptians and Romans had great gardens but the Greeks did not own private gardens. They decorated walkways and roads with statues. The pleasure gardens exhibiting wealth were surprisingly absent during Greek period. The Hellenismus developed different forms of art and architecture influencing its many and famous gardens. The contacts that the Hellenistic world had with the Egyptians and the Mesopotamic gardeners were very important. We know them only through the literary sources which are very schematic. Alexandria had beautiful parks covering a quarter of the ancient town's area. In Alexandria, as in Greece, gardens were set near the town's walls. Those gardens were connected encircling the town in a large green belt. Most beautiful were also the gardens of Antiochia, the Seleucids' capital. This town was cut in two by a colonnaded road. On one side stood the buildings and on the other the gardens were adorned by pavilions, baths, fountains and park. All the literary descriptions do not help to understand the Hellenistic garden. However, in Rhodes, it is still possible to visit places dedicated to Nymphs. In ancient times they were well arranged and decorated by green plants with sculptures. It is a kind of garden landscaping totally free from the rigid geometric schemes. Roman copies of the Hellenistic gardens can be seen in the Museums. All the statues were set on natural or artificial rocks and placed near the gardens with water reflections. Everything imitated the nature rather than the symmetry.

D. Roman gardens

Roman gardens were a place of peace and quietness. Ornamental horticulture developed during the evolution of Roman civilisation. The administrators of the Roman Empire (c.100 BC - 500 AD) exchanged information on agriculture, horticulture, animal husbandry, hydraulics, and botany. Seeds and plants were widely shared. The *Gardens of Lucullus* (Horti Lucullani) on the *Pincian Hill* on the edge of Rome introduced the Persian garden to Europe around 60 BC. The green spaces in and around Rome were tended as either wild hunting woods or vegetable patches until the fall of the Roman Empire.

E. Byzantium Gardens

The Byzantine Empire spanned a period of more than 1000 years (330-1453 AD). It had a geographical area of the present day Spain and Britain to the Middle East and North Africa. There is no single dominant garden style called as "Byzantine style" due to this large geographic area and its turbulent history.

Archaeological evidence of public, imperial and private gardens is not clear. Researchers relied on literary sources to find the main features of Byzantine gardens. Romantic novels of the 12th century included detailed descriptions of gardens. Their popularity shows the Byzantine enthusiasm for pleasure gardens. Formal gardening texts of the 10th century were encyclopedias of collected agricultural practices going back to *Hesiod's* time. Their repeated publications and translations to other languages up to the 16th century shows the value attributed to the horticultural knowledge. These books promoted the concepts of walled gardens with plants arranged by type. Such ideals found expression in the suburban parks *(Philopation, Aretai)* and palatial gardens (*Mesokepion, Mangana)* of Constantinople

The Byzantine garden tradition was influenced by the empire history. The first major influence was the adoption of Christianity as the empire's official religion by its founder Constantine-I. Second major influence after the 9th century was the contact with the Islamic nations of the Middle East with lavish furnishings and the adoption of automatic devices in the palatial gardens. Third major influence was a fundamental shift in the design of the Byzantine cities after the 7th century when they became small in size and population. Wealthy aristocrats reduced in number who could maintain elaborate gardens. The last major influence was a trend dominant in Europe of an enclosed garden space. The open views and vistas favoured by the garden builders of the Roman villas were replaced by garden walls painted with scenic views inside. The concept of the heavenly paradise was an enclosed garden.

Monasteries practiced horticulture during the long history of Byzantine period. This is evident in the foundation documents of many Christian monasteries and the biographies of saints describing their gardening activities. Monasteries maintained gardens outside their walls and watered them with irrigation systems fed by springs or rainwater. These gardens contained vineyards, vegetables and fruit trees for monks and pilgrims. Monks played the role of the gardeners as a service. These horticultural practices are still in use in Christian monasteries in Greece and the Middle East.

F. Chinese and Japanese gardens

Traditionally Chinese and Japanese garden design is intended to invoke the natural landscape of mountains and rivers. However, the viewpoint of the gardens differs: Chinese gardens were intended to be viewed from within the garden and as a setting for everyday life. Japanese gardens, with a few exceptions, were intended to be viewed from within the house, sort of like a diorama. Chinese gardens often included a water feature, while Japanese gardens set in a wetter climate would often deal with the suggestion of water such as sand or pebbles raked into a wave pattern. Traditional Chinese gardens treat the plants in a naturalistic way, while traditional Japanese gardens feature plants cut into mountain shapes. These contrasts with the handling of stone elements: in a Japanese garden, stones are placed in groupings as part of the landscape, but in a Chinese garden, a particularly choice stone might even be placed on a pedestal in a prominent location so that it might be more easily appreciated.

G. Chinese scholar gardens

The style of Chinese garden varies among economic groups and differs by dynasties. Rocks, water, bridges and pavilions are the most common features of scholar gardens for the wealthy classes. Courtyards, wells, and terra cotta fish tanks are common among general population. Other features such as moon gates and openwork screens piercing surrounding walls are seen in both groups.

There are two ways of looking at the signature design characteristics of the Chinese garden: first, the concept of *Yin* and *Yang* and second, the myths of longevity that arose during the *Qin* Dynasty.

The philosophy of *Yin* and *Yang* portrays the idea of balance and harmony. The Chinese garden expresses the relationship to nature and the idea of balance through the art of imitating natural setting, thus the existence of mountains, rocks, water and wind elements. *Yin* and *Yang* place complementary opposites: as hard as rock can be, the softness of water can dissolve it. *Tai Hu* rocks, limestone eroded by the water of Lake *Tai*, are the typical example. Water, air and light run through the rock as it sit still on display. The screen windows of the Chinese garden wall portray both steadiness and movement. The windows create a solid painting on walls; however that steadiness changes once the wind blows or the eyes move.

Chinese garden's structure is based upon the culture's creation myth, rooted in rocks and water. To have longevity is to live among mountains and water. It is to live with nature and live like an immortal being (*Xian*). The garden evokes a healthy lifestyle making one immortal, free from the problems of civilization. Thus, Chinese landscape is known as *Shan* (mountain) and *Shui* (water).

Symbolism is a key element of Chinese garden design. To the earthy tones of the Chinese garden, a touch of red or gold is often added to bring forth the *Yin/Yang* contrast. The colors red and gold also represent luck and wealth. Bats, dragons and other mystic creatures carved on wooden doors are also commonly found in Chinese gardens. These are signs of luck and protection. Circles portray togetherness, especially for family members. They are depicted in moon gates and round tables placed within square backgrounds. The moon gate and other fanciful doorways also act to frame views and to force the viewer to pause for a transition into a new space. Paths in Chinese gardens are often uneven and sometimes consciously zigzag. These paths are like the passages of a human life. There is always something new or different when seen from a different angle, while the future is unknown and unpredictable.

Fig 2.10. Penjing Garden, pagoda Yunyan Ta, China

Fig 2.11. Administrator's Garden, China

Fig 2.12. Blossom in Nanjing, China

H. European gardens

1. Medieval

Monasteries carried on a tradition of garden design and strong horticultural techniques during the medieval period in Europe. The variety of different purposes the garden monasteries had serves as testament to their sophistication rather than any one particular horticultural technique employed. Records are limited as far as gardening practices are concerned. There are no existing monastic gardens which are entirely true to original form. However, records and plans indicate the types of garden a monastery might have had, such as those for St. Gall in Switzerland.

Generally, monastic garden types consisted of kitchen gardens, hospital gardens, cemetery orchards and vineyards. Individual monasteries might also have had a "green court," a plot of grass and trees where horses could graze. Private gardens were provided for monks, who held specific posts within the monastery.

Vegetable and herb gardens helped provide both nourishing and medicinal crops, which could be used to feed or treat the monks and the outside community. As detailed in the plans for St. Gall, these gardens were laid out in rectangular plots, with narrow paths between them to facilitate collection of yields. Often these beds were surrounded with fencing to prevent animals from entry. In the kitchen gardens: fennel, cabbage, onion, garlic, leeks, radishes, parsnips, peas, lentils and beans was grown. The hospital gardens could contain savory, costmary, fenugreek, rosemary, peppermint, rue, iris, sage, bergamot, mint, lovage, fennel and cumin. The herb and vegetable gardens served a purpose beyond that of production. Their installation and maintenance allowed the monks to fulfill the manual labor component of the religious way of life prescribed by Rule of St. Benedict.

Orchards also served as sites for food production and as arenas for manual labor. Cemetery orchards like St. Gall showed more versatility. The cemetery orchard not only produced fruit, but manifested as a natural symbol of the garden of Paradise. This bi-fold concept of the garden as a space that met both physical and spiritual needs was carried over to the religious residence.

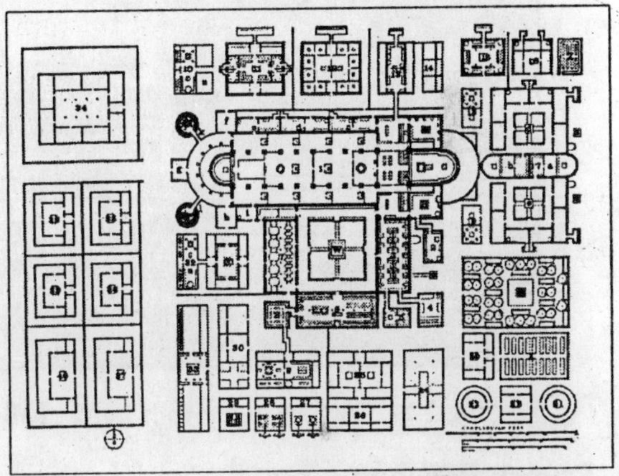

Fig 2.13. St.Gall Plan of monastery, Switzerland

The viridarium was often cut by paths featured a roofed fountain at the center or side of the garth serving as a primary source for wash water and for irrigation. Some cloister gardens contained small fish ponds as another source of food for the community. The arcades were used for teaching, sitting and meditating or for exercise in rough weather.This tendency to instill the garden with symbolic values was not inherent to the religious orders alone, but was a feature of medieval culture in general. The square closter garth was meant to represent the four points of the compass. While meditating, walking around the cloister was a way of devoting to the path of life. Each of the monastic gardens was filled with symbolic as well as tangible value, testifying to the ingenuity of its creators.

In the later Middle Ages, texts, art and literary works provide a picture of developments in garden design. During the late 12th to 15th centuries, European cities were walled for internal defense and to control trade. Though space within these walls was limited, surviving documents show that there were animals, fruit trees and kitchen gardens inside the city limits.

Pietro Crescenzi, a Bolognese lawyer, wrote twelve volumes on the practical aspects of farming in the 13th century. They offer a description of medieval gardening practices. Gardens were surrounded with stonewalls, thick hedging or fencing and incorporated trellises and arbors. They borrowed their form from the square or rectangular shape of the cloister and included square planting beds. Grass was first noticed in the medieval garden. Raised banks covered in turf called "Turf Seats" were constructed to provide seating in the garden. Fruit trees were prevalent and often grafted to produce new varieties of fruit. Gardens included a raised mound or mount to serve as a stage for viewing and planting beds. Two works from the late Middle Ages discuss plant cultivation. In the English poem "The Feate of Gardinage" by Jon Gardener and the general household advice given in Le Ménagier de Paris of 1393, a variety of herbs, flowers, fruit trees and bushes were listed with instructions on their cultivation. The Menagier provides advice by season on sowing, planting and grafting. The most sophisticated gardening during the Middle Ages was done at the monasteries. Monks developed horticultural techniques and cultivated herbs, fruits and vegetables. Monks treated those suffering inside the monastery and surrounding communities using the medicinal herbs they grew. During the Middle Ages, gardens were thought to unite the earthly with the divine. Enclosed gardens were often depicted in the visual arts, picturing the Virgin Mary, a fountain, a unicorn and roses inside an enclosed area for religious and spiritual significance. Though Medieval gardens lacked many of the features of the Renaissance gardens that followed them, some of the characteristics of these gardens continue to be incorporated today.

2. Italian Renaissance

The Italian Renaissance inspired a revolution in gardening. Renaissance gardens were full of scenes from ancient mythology. Water was especially symbolic. It was associated with fertility and the abundance of nature. The Medici Villa Petraia, near Florence by Niccolò Tribolo symbolizes the Italian garden of the early Renaissance before the grander architectural schemes of the 16th century Gardens of the French Renaissance.

Fig 2.14. Gardens of the Villa Lante, Italy

Fig 2.15. Palazzo Piccolomini at Pienza, Italy

Fig 2.16. Villa di Castello, Florence, Italy

3. French Baroque

The French Classical garden style culminated during the reign of Louis XIV of France (1638-1715) and his head gardener of Versailles, André Le Nôtre (1613-1700). The inspiration for these gardens initially came from the Italian Renaissance garden of the 14th and 15th centuries and ideas of French philosopher Renée Descartes (1576-1650).

The French opened the garden to enormous proportions compared to their Italian predecessor. Their gardens show man dominating and manipulating nature to show his authority, wealth, and power. Renée Descartes, the founder of analytical geometry, believed that the natural world was objectively measurable and that space is infinitely divisible.

Fig 2.17. Villa Medici a Fiesole, Florence, Italy

The formal and symmetrical garden style placed the house centrally on a huge and mainly flat property. A large central axis that gets narrower from the main house compels the viewer's perspective making the property look even larger. The viewer can see the property as a whole but unable to see all the components of the garden. One is to be led through a logical progression or story and be surprised by elements not visible until approached. There is a symbolic story referring to the owner through statues and water features with mythological references. There are small, hardly noticeable grade changes concealing the gardens surprises and stretch the gardens views.

4. Picturesque gardens

The picturesque garden style emerged in England in the 18th century. Garden designers like William Kent and Capability Brown copied the landscape paintings of European artists Claude Lorraine, Poussin and Salvator Rosa. The groomed hills, lakes and trees dotted with temples were sculpted into the land.

By the 1790s there was a reaction against these stereotyped compositions. Number of thinkers began to promote the idea of picturesque gardens. The leader of the movement was landscape theorist William Gilpin, an accomplished artist known for his realistic depictions of nature. He chose the natural landscape to the topography of a given site. He felt that while classical beauty was linked with the smooth and neat features, picturesque beauty had a wilder, untamed quality. The picturesque style also incorporated castles, Gothic ruins, rustic cottages to add interest and depth to the landscape

Controversy between the picturesque school and exponents of groomed garden continued into the 19th century. Landscape designer Humphrey Repton supported Gilpin's ideas of the garden harmonizing with surrounding landforms. Repton showed the differences between painting and landscape gardening. The viewer moves through garden constantly shifting viewpoints unlike a painting.

The French landscape garden was separate from contemporary English gardens. Rococo features like Turkish tents and Chinese bridges were prevalent in French gardens in the 18th century. The French Picturesque garden style falls into two categories: one that is almost rustic and exotic like theatrical scenery, and the other filled with pastoral romance and peasant sentiment. The former style is represented by the Parc Monceau, the latter by the Moulin Jolie. The rusticity found in French Picturesque gardens is derived from an admiration of Dutch 17th century landscape painting and works of French 18th century artists.

5. 'Gardenesque' gardens

The 'Gardenesque' style of English garden design evolved during the 1820s largely under the influence of J. C. Loudon, who invented the term. In a Gardenesque plan, all the trees, shrubs and other plants are positioned and managed to display the character of each plant to its full potential. The Gardenesque plan tended to emphasize botanical curiosities and a collector's approach with the spread of botany as a suitable hobby. The Gardenesque approach involved the creation of small-scale landscapes with features to promote beauty of detail, variety and mystery. Artificial mounds and island beds became prominent features.

Fig. 2.18. Typical Picturisque garden

Fig. 2.19. Typical Gardenisque garden

Fig. 2.20. Typical Industrial garden

6. Modern gardens

In the 20th century, modern garden design became important as architects began to design buildings and residences with an eye toward innovation, problem solving and removing unnecessary ornamentation. Garden design followed in the same philosophy of form following function of buildings. Garrett Eckbo, James Rose, and Dan Kiley, who met while studying traditional landscape architecture at Harvard University, became notable pioneers in the design of modern gardens. They became interested in developing functional space for outdoor living with designs depicting natural surroundings. Modern gardens feature a fresh mix of curved and linier designs and many include abstract art in geometrics and sculpture. Spaces are defined with the thoughtful placement of trees and plantings. Frank Lloyd Wright also presented his version for the modern garden by designing homes in complete harmony with natural surroundings. Taliesin and Fallingwater are both examples of careful placement of architecture in nature, so the relationship between the residence and surroundings become seamless.

Fig. 2.21. Typical Modern garden

I. Indian gardens:

Not much is known about the ancient gardens in India. The oldest stone buildings in India were made at Harappa in the lower Indus valley. Their script has not been decoded, so it is not known whether the small outdoor courts in their cities contained plants or not. The Harappans set up streets on a grid plan and formed courtyard houses. There is no archaeological evidence of early gardens elsewhere in India. The ancient Hindu sacred books give a detailed account of gardens in ancient India. Europe has more archaeological evidence of its ancient gardens but less textual evidence. The fertile plains of India were forested and buildings were relatively temporary structures in timber and mud. *Hindu* palace and garden construction has not survived.

Mauryan civilisation under the rule of *Ashoka* (269-232 BC) converted to *Buddhism* and built religious structures in stone. Stupas representing *Buddha* tomb were placed in fenced enclosures. The *Mauryan's* also built palaces. There is a Greek description of a palace set amongst gardens at Patna. It had open halls and wooden columns. The Hindu scriptures set down a code for the orientation and organisation of buildings in relation to compass points, hills, water and plants. Enclosed outdoor space in the form of courtyards became essential to housing in India. Town dwellings had rooms grouped around a courtyard. Old palace buildings are not surviving now, but rock carvings show airy structures with timber columns. The illustrations at Ajanta caves show plants in front and rear side of the platform and columns.

From the 12th century onwards, India was occupied by Arabs, Turks and Mughals. They came from the west and north bringing new religion of Islam, new weapons and new building techniques.

Fig. 2.22. Amber fort gardens, Jaipur, India

In India, the Mughal innovation was to treat the enclosed outdoor space of tombs as a garden. The tomb garden became a model. The three types of gardens made by the Mughals were:

1. tomb gardens
2. palace gardens
3. camp gardens

Fig. 2.23. Lodi garden, Delhi, India

Each type of garden was conceived as the making of an earthly paradise in an Islamic context. The *Rajputs,* a warrior class, retained their power during the periods of *Mughal* and European influence. The style of their palaces and gardens became partly Hindu and partly foreign-influenced. The classic Indian townhouse and farmhouse rooms opened onto a courtyard with a wall to give protection from the outside world. Palace forts had strong fortifications and specialised courtyards for men, women, relatives, guests, cooking and horses. Under Muslim influence and prosperity, courtyards developed into paradise gardens. This development led garden design playing a significant part in palace layout.

As European influence on India became significant, several factors contributed to a new wave of palace building. There was a building boom from the 18th century onwards led by Indian princes. Portuguese and French influence was strong in South India. The British built large estates for their own use. The new palaces built were a mix of *Mughal* and *Rajput* influences. As the 19th century progressed European influence became stronger, but Indian buildings and gardens retained their character.

Fig. 2.24. Jahaj-mahal-garden, Mandu, India

Fig 2.25 Udaipur Garden, Udaipur, India

EXERCISE

1. What are the main design features of the following ancient gardens?
   (*a*) Persian gardens
   (*b*) Egyptian gardens
2. What are the main design features of the following ancient gardens?
   (*a*) Hellenistic gardens
   (*b*) Roman gardens
   (*c*) Byzantium Gardens
4. Compare the design features of ancient Chinese and Japanese gardens.
5. What are the major features of ancient European gardens?
6. What are the major features of ancient Indian gardens?

3

Basics of Landscape Design

The basic concept of landscape design is to create attractive and functional outdoor spaces for different uses by using horticultural science, aesthetic composition and spatial organization. The elements and principles are used to create spaces visually pleasing to the eye. The design process begins by determining the needs and desires of the user and the conditions of the site. The most efficient, functional and aesthetically pleasing landscape should be developed to satisfy the needs of the people who will use and maintain it. The planting design should be compatible with the existing environmental conditions. The design should enhance the quality of life for the users. Good landscape design and the arrangement and placement of plants are all based on certain plant characteristics and time-tested design principles. The visual characteristics of plant size, form, texture, and colour contribute to the functional and aesthetic qualities of a planting design.

Plant size should be the primary consideration. Large plants, such as shade trees, should be located first; the smaller trees, shrubs, and finally the ground covers should be arranged to provide a sense of support or framework to the overall design. Shade and evergreen trees, such as maples or spruce, are the most dominant plants in the landscape design. They provide background, visual weight and structural framework. Ornamental trees, such as flowering crabapples and birches, are used as focal points or dominant elements because of their seasonal and picturesque branching characteristics. Tall shrubs help establish vertical edges to an outdoor space, create screens, enhance privacy, or provide a neutral background. Small shrubs are also used to define edges and spaces without blocking views; they can connect and link unrelated or separate plants, and define areas and space on the ground.

The features of a landscape can be physically described by the visual qualities or the elements of design. The principles are the fundamental concepts of composition to organize the features to create a beautiful landscape.

A. Elements of design

1. **Form:** It is an important consideration in a planting composition. The most common plant shapes are the spreading and rounded forms. These two basic plant forms have the most application in planting design; they create neutral patterns in contrast with more unusual forms of plants. Columnar and pyramidal-shaped plants have visual characteristics that suggest vertical edges in an outdoor space. They create a major contrast with the more common rounded or spreading plants. The picturesque and drooping forms of plants are useful as accents or focal points in the planting design when used sparingly. Common plant forms are well

established. Form is the steady characteristic of plants. Form can also be created through the massing of plants. The overall mass creates a different form than an individual plant. A contrast form within the composition will have greater emphasis. Natural plant forms should create the size of the composition. The significance of overall form depends on the viewing place. Vertical forms add height, horizontal forms add width.

Form is also the main determining factor of a formal or informal garden. Geometric forms with straight edges are typical of formal gardens. They are based on an established style. An informal garden has more naturalistic, organic forms. They are normally found in gardens imitating nature. Form compatibility is also a major component of unity in design. One or two striking forms are good for contrast and emphasis, but generally all other forms should have some similarities for a unified look.

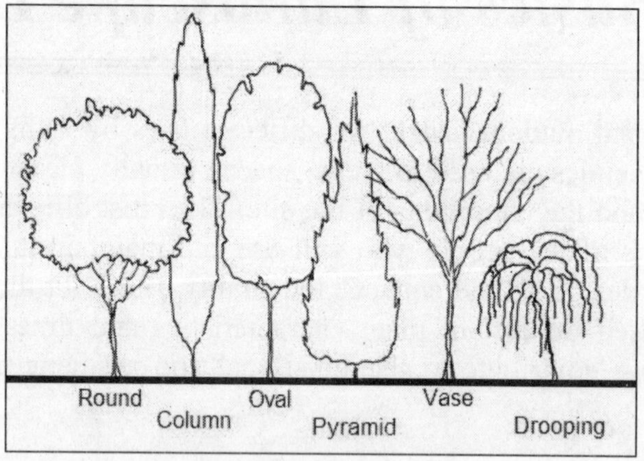

Fig. 3.1. Different plant forms

Fig. 3.2. Drooping tree form

2. **Texture:** It refers to the visual roughness or smoothness of a plant. The texture of the foliage, twigs and branches is coarse, medium or fine. Texture effects are most visible at close range and in smaller landscape plantings. Coarse-textured plants tend to be dominant and attract attention. They usually have dense foliage or broad leaves. Fine-textured plants appear delicate and tend to recede from view. They usually have fine foliage or needle leaves. In planting composition, medium-textured plants should dominate and contrast with either the coarse or fine textures.

   A plant can generally have a coarse, medium or fine texture. Plant characteristics that create coarse texture are leaves with very irregular edges, varied colors and thick branches. Most plants are medium texture because they cannot be described as having either coarse or fine texture. They are characterized by medium-sized leaves with simple shapes and smooth edges. The average-sized branches are not densely spaced nor widely spaced. Characteristics that create fine texture are small foliage, thin leaves, thin stems, tiny twigs, long stems and delicate flowers.

   Texture affects the view of distance and scale. To make a space appear larger, locate plants of fine textures along the outer perimeter, the medium textures in the middle and the coarse textures near the viewer. To make a space appear smaller, place the coarse textures along the outer perimeter and the fine textures near the viewer. Bold colors increase the contrast and the texture appears coarser, while soft colors flatten texture.

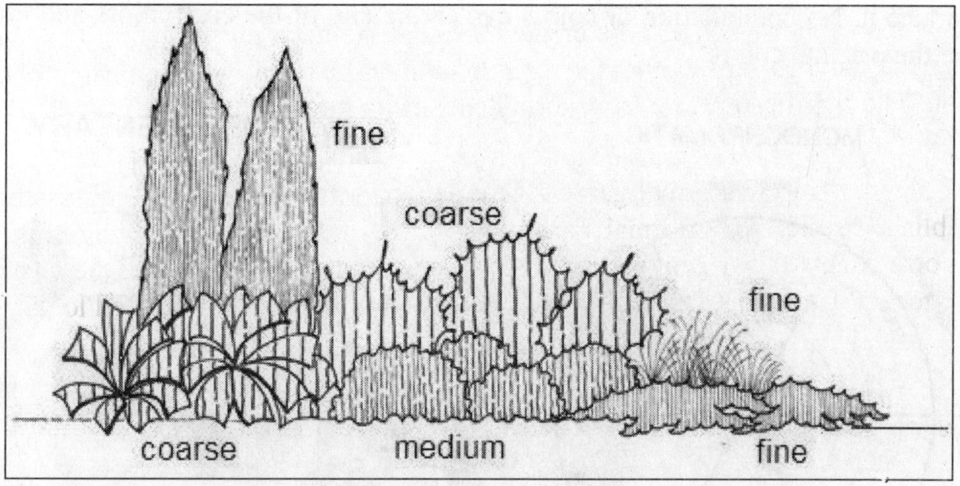

Fig. 3.3. Different plant textures

Fig. 3.4. Plant textures in a garden

3. **Color:** It is one of the most visual plant characteristics. It includes the Color of leaves, flowers, fruit, branches, and bark. Green is the predominant plant color, but has seasonal variations. With evergreens, the same color is present year round. The color of the summer foliage has the longest seasonal effect and the most importance in design composition. A variety of greens have more visual appeal when displayed against a uniform neutral green background. A common mistake is to use too many different colors. Plant color can be used as an attractor, to call attention to some area in the landscape. Dark-coloured plants contrasted with light-coloured plants create focal points in a planting composition. Nature is in colour. Light is source of all colors. We react emotionally to different colors in different ways. Color has the power to influence and brings out the feelings. For example, bright colors create a sense of joy and happiness. Dark and gloomy colors create a sense of sadness and fear.

Plants should be arranged for summer foliage effects first, and then color characteristics of flowers, fall foliage, fruit, or branching. Foliage color varies with texture. Fine-textured leaves are more reflective and tend to be weaker in overall visual effect. Plant colors can also be used to suggest certain emotional or psychological feelings. Dark greens give a somber, gloomy feeling. Lighter greens suggest gaiety and cheerfulness.

There are 3 dominant groups of colours in the colour wheel:

1. Primary colors,
2. Secondary colors and
3. Intermediate colors.

Primary Colors

The Primary Colors are the main colors. They are always seen as the strongest and powerful colors and these are used in logos and posters to make energy and strong statements. The primary colors are Red, Blue and Yellow. These three are the core colors which cannot be generated by mixing other colors together to produce it. No combination of colors can create any of the core colors and thus they are known as the primary colors simply because they are the original colors

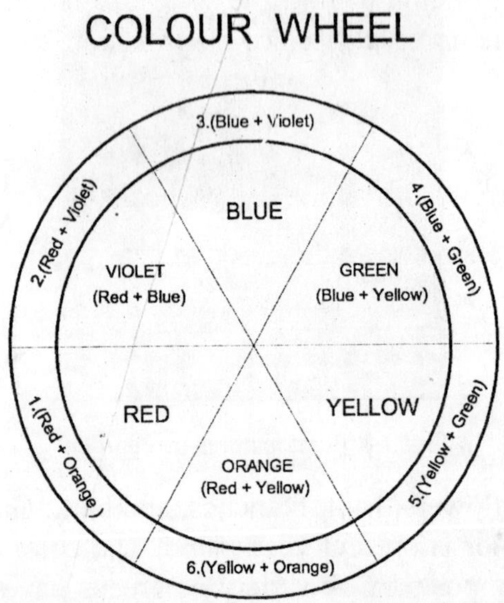

Fig. 3.5. Colour wheel

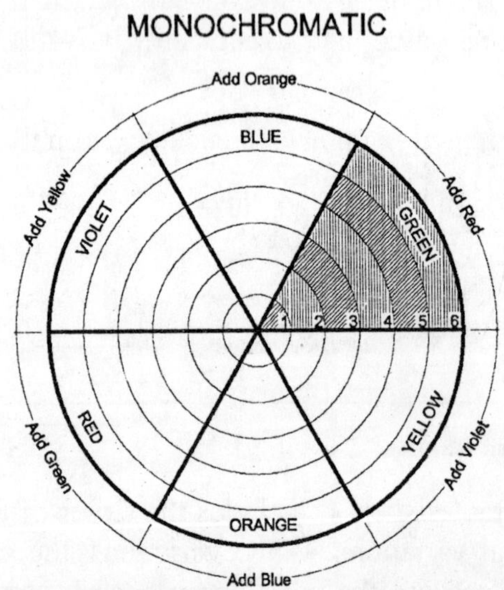

Fig. 3.6. Monochromatic

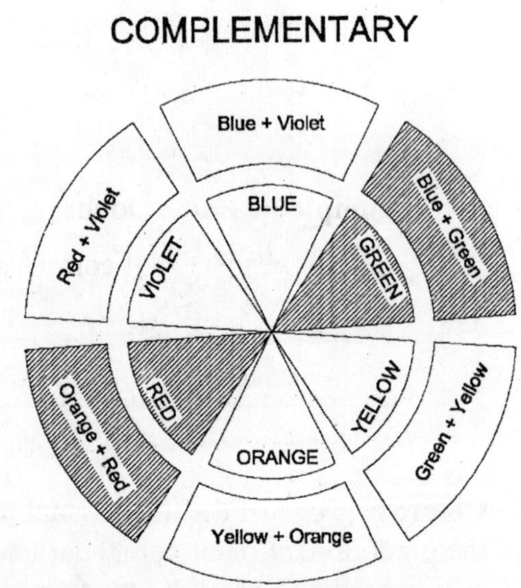

Fig. 3.7. Complementary

Secondary Colors

Secondary Colors are the combination of the primary colors to produce another color. There are 3 secondary colors: orange, purple and green. Orange is the product of mixing yellow + red, Purple/ indigo is the mix of blue + red, and green is the product of blue + yellow. The mixture ratios for the colors are equal.

Intermediate or Tertiary Colours

Intermediate Colours are made from combining the secondary and the primer colors together and usually with the color next to one another. There are 6 Intermediate colours, light green: green + yellow, Light orange: Orange + Yellow, orange red: red + orange, violet: purple + Red, indigo: blue + purple, dark Green: blue + green. The Intermediate colors create a sense of softness and have the ability to lower the intensity of the primer and secondary colors if they are used together in a good composition.

Contrast color schemes

There are 6 groups of contrast color schemes:

1. Monochromatic,
2. Complementary,
3. Double complementary,
4. Split complementary,

5. Triad and
6. Tetrad

1. **Monochromatic**: Monochromatic colors are made out of one color but in different tones ranging from the softest to the darkest tone. The more white is used to lower the tone value, and to increase the value black is used. This color composition creates a harmonious and comfortable feeling.
2. **Complementary**: Complementary colors are directly opposite to each other on the color wheel.
3. **Double complementary**: Double complementary color consists of a pair of complementary colors on the color wheel.
4. **Split complementary**: Split complementary colors consist of two colors that join its complements on the color wheel.

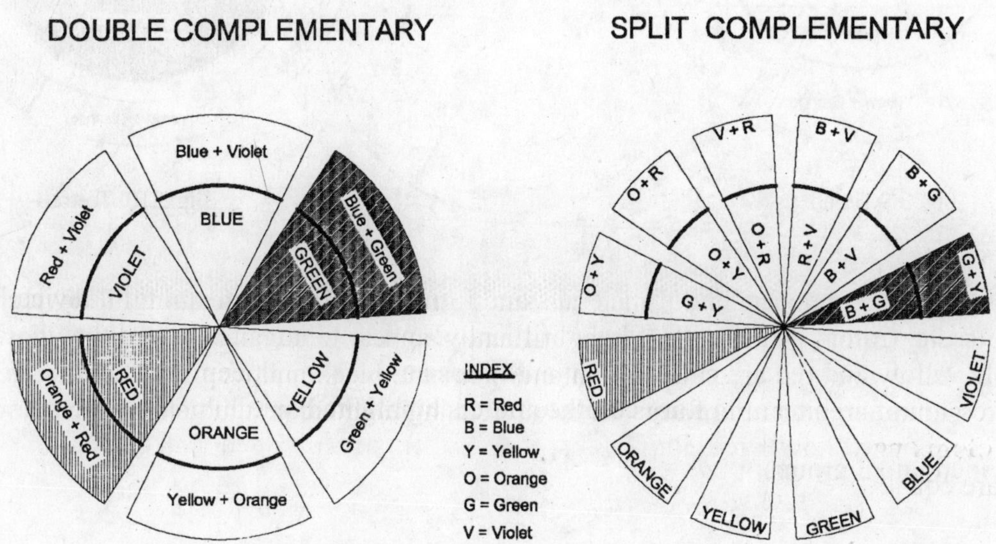

Fig. 3.8. Double complementary and Split complementary colours

5. **Triad**: Triad color scheme combines three colors obtained by placing an equilateral triangle on the color wheel. By rotating the triangle on the color wheel different combinations can be obtained.
6. **Tetrad:** Tetrad colour scheme is obtained by any four colours on the colour wheel, which are adjacent to one another.

Color has three dimensions:

1. the hue, means color such as red, green, blue
2. the tone or intensity, means the brightness or dullness
3. the value, means lightness or darkness

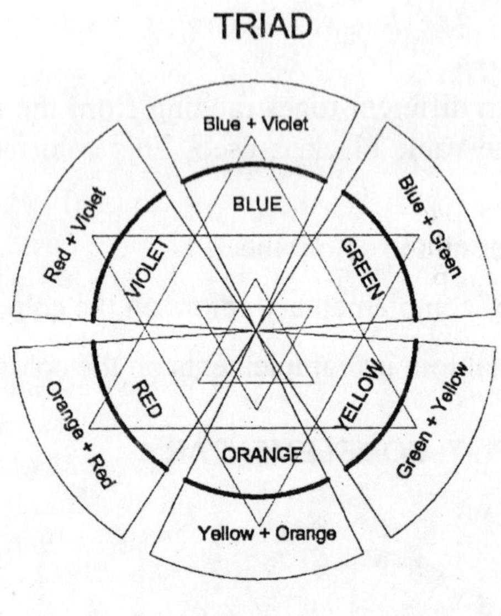

Fig. 3.9. Triad

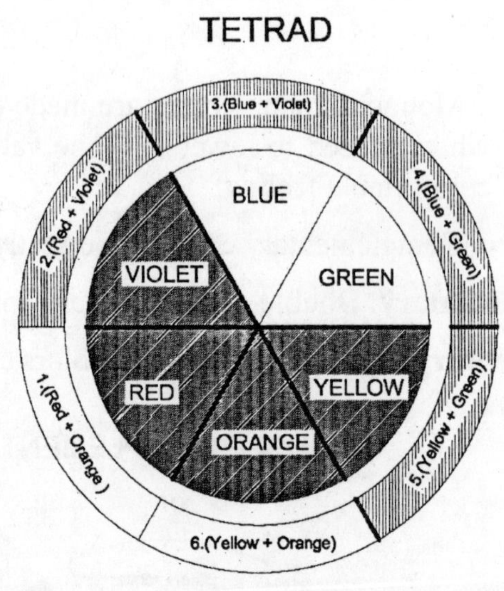

Fig. 3.10. Tetrad

Color Value

The values associated with color are independent of materials and forms. A different meaningful device is provided by the great range of light reflection in the color scale. Colors, which reflect light brilliantly, appear to advance toward the viewer, and those that absorb light appear to recede. For example yellow and red are called bright and pleasant, black and deep blue colors are called dark and gloomy. The degree of projection and depression of architectural forms can be altered, highlighted or subdued by the colors of their surfaces.

The value of colors is divided into 3 groups:

1. Color tones,
2. Chromo colors, and
3. Neutral colors

1. Color Tones: Color tones are the effects of the light beams from the brightest to the darkest. It's the same with tonal colors, where white and black are used to create different color values. The lightest value contains more white and the darkest contains the most black. Color tones are very important and useful in producing three- dimensional spaces.

2. Chromo Colors: Chromo colors are the creation from mixing two contrast colors in certain ratios, which creates a tonal value flowing from the two colors. Chromo colors create a dull color from the original colors, which are used to show dark and gloomy side of life.

3. Neutral Colors: Neutral colors are black and white. They are neutral because they have no strength and power, but yet they can increase or decrease the value of colors. These two colors have value when mixed together and the tone value change from white to

black. White turns into grey and finally into black. Neutral colors also mean chromo colors because the creation from both mixtures produces colors which have lost the originality of its core colors. Neutral colors can create a comfortable and less stressing environment.

4. **Line:** Line in the landscape is created by the edge between two materials of a long linear feature. Lines can be used to create many varieties of shapes and forms. They control movement of the eye and the body. Landscape designers use lines to create patterns, spaces, forms and an organized theme in a landscape. Three primary line types create form in the landscape: bed lines, hardscape and plants. Bed lines are created where the edge of the plant bed meets another surface material, such as turf, groundcover, gravel, or patio pavers. Hardscape lines are created by the edge of the hardscape. Plants are used to create different shapes of lines. Line can also be created by long and narrow materials like a fence or wall.

   Lines should be dramatic, done with a sense of flamboyancy and be very expressive in their shape in curvilinear design. Curvilinear lines that have weak edges will not be visually interesting or pleasing to the eye. Curvilinear, meandering lines suggest a naturalistic look that invites the user to casually stroll through and experience the landscape. On the other hand, linear lines such as those found in a straight hedge or the edges of paving materials suggest quick, direct movement. Angled lines can create opportunities for creating the "bones or the framework of the landscape". Lines that interconnect at right angles create an opportunity for reflection, stopping or sitting. Through skillful use of lines in the landscape, the designer is able to direct the attention of the viewer to a focal point.

Fig. 3.11. Line

Fig. 3.12. Scale

5. **Scale & Proportion:** Good proportion and scale have no hard and fast rules. Scale can be understood most simply as relative size. Scale usually bears reference to the size of a thing or object that appears to have a pleasing relationship to other things or to the design as a whole. It essentially relates to some finite measure of universal application or a standard of known dimension.

Proportion is the relationship of the width to the length of an area or the relationship to parts of an organization. Relative proportion is the size of an object in relation to other objects. Absolute proportion is the scale or size of an object. An important absolute scale in design is the human scale (size of the human body) because the size of other objects is considered relative to humans. Plant material, garden structures and ornaments should be considered relative to human scale. Human scale, on the other hand, refers to the relationship between the size of composition and the observer. Other important relative proportion is the area to be planted. The fixed parameters of the garden decide to some extent how spaces and patterns can be used. A long, thin garden needs to be handled in a different way than a rectangular, square or triangular garden. A long and narrow garden can improve by breaking its length into separate spaces. A garden may appear longer by establishing a long axis.

B. Principles of design

1. **Unity:** Unity is achieved by linking elements and features to create a consistent character in the composition. Scattered groupings of plants and unrelated garden ornaments are the opposite of unity. Hardscapes and plants can be unified by blending similar characteristics, but some variety is also important to create interest. The simplest way to create unity is through the use of a design theme or a design style. Unity may also be obtained by restricting a garden to a certain class of plants—perennials, roses, or annuals.

   Unity in design can be achieved by reducing the number of different elements such as plant species, sizes, forms, colors or textures. A basic principle in planting design is to group plants together in groups of three, five or seven rather than scattering them. Young plants may first appear as small individuals, but as they grow and mature they should be viewed as a group unless they are designed as individual specimens. Scattered plants or groups of plants can be connected with beds of ground covers or low shrubs. A simple experiment will indicate whether the design has unity. Cover up certain elements in the design; a bed or border or a group of plants. See whether the design suffers because of the exclusion. If not, the part covered is unnecessary.

2. **Balance**: Balance is the concept of equal visual attraction and weight on central axis. Balance is either formal (symmetrical) or informal (asymmetrical) in nature. Formal balance is achieved when the same objects are placed on either side of an imaginary axis. Many historic gardens are organized using this concept. In formal balance, the mass or weight or numbers of objects on either side of a central axis should be exactly the same. Plants are frequently clipped, lines tend to be straight and edges are clearly defined. Informal balance is achieved by equal visual weight of different forms, color or texture on either side of an axis. The mass can be achieved by combinations of plants, structures and garden ornaments. Plants should be irregularly placed on either side of an imaginary axis so that the mass or weight on either side of the axis appears to be balanced. Curved lines, obscure and merging edges and natural contours identify asymmetry in the garden.

3. **Focal point:** Dominant features that capture attention are called focal points. Focal points are used to draw attention to a particular location. They are the features or objects in a garden that draw the eye and lead the visitor towards them. They play a pivotal role both in movement round the garden and in the composition as a whole. It suggests that one element in the composition has authority over other subordinate parts. Dominance may be created by size like a shade tree or by form, texture, color or location of the elements within a design. The dominant element becomes the focal point. Major contrast is a similar design principle where one element is so different that other parts of the composition are subordinated to that element, such as a bed of red salvia flowers against a background of green yews. Garden ornaments also attract attention because they are often different from plant material.

Form and color are usually contrasting the most with plants. Sculptures, planters and furniture have forms which are easily different from plants. A focal point can be carried out in a number of ways, such as:

- a dramatic fountain at the end of an avenue
- the perfect positioning of a simple garden pot at the end of a wall
- a pot or obelisk in a formal setting
- a bench under a rose-covered trellis
- a mound swinging under an apple tree
- a piece of sculpture half hidden in a border
- a gate leading out of the garden to the landscape beyond
- a pool set to catch a reflection.

A garden can only support a certain number of focal points. A small garden should have only one. A large garden can have a few more, if they are sited in different areas. A single object in well positioned place is always more effective. The important factor is that the focal point should attract for some purpose. It can be to divert from the area passing through, to lead on to some other view or some other part of the garden.

Fig. 3.13. Unity

Fig. 3.14. Balance

Fig. 3.15. Focal point

1. **Repetition and rhythm:** Repetition is created by the repeated use of elements or features to create patterns or a sequence in the landscape. Repeating line, form, color and texture creates rhythm in the landscape. Simple repetition is the use of the same object in a line or geometric form like a square in an organized pattern. They are planting design principles achieved when similar plant characteristics are introduced and repeated to help create the feeling of recall or unity in the composition. Interconnection is a

principle similar to repetition whereby different plants are linked together by overlapping or touching similar plants. Fences, walls or beds of ground cover are frequently used to link elements together in the landscape.

2. **Transition**: The effective use of sequence is often employed to create visual movement in the landscape. It is an important consideration to take into account in the development of the overall planting pattern. For example, sequence could be an orderly natural combination of plant material. In this case, low objects would appear in the foreground, intermediate objects in the middle ground and tall objects in the background.

Fig. 3.16. Rhythm

Fig. 3.17. Repetition

Fig. 3.18. Transition

The **theme** of a planting composition may be informal, curved or natural. The style may give a formal, linear or symmetrical theme. By following a definite order or style, the design does not have a fragmented or uncoordinated appearance. The most visually pleasing designs are not created by chance, but follow a specific order, theme or style which carries throughout the landscape.

C. Plant Selection

1. **Mature size and proper spacing:** Many plants are available in different varieties. These varieties often vary in mature size, flower color and leaf appearance.

2. **Long or short life:** Plants vary in their life span. People who love to work in the garden and enjoy change will prefer short-lived plants like perennials. Those who want a landscape that gets installed and then needs minimal care need to consider this when choosing their plants.

3. **Evergreen and deciduous:** Most people want plants that don't lose their leaves (evergreens). However, there are certain advantages to deciduous trees. For example, maybe it's best that patio trees provide shade in the summer and allow the sun to heat things up in the winter. However care should be taken because some trees lose their leaves in the spring, not the winter (jacaranda and tipu tree for example).

4. **Potential root damage:** Do not plant large trees too close to a sidewalk, driveway or the house. Plants vary in their potential to cause root damage.

5. **Pests and diseases:** It's not a good idea to plant something that has constant pest problems. This is something that changes frequently as foreign insect and disease invasions occur.

6. **Weather conditions:** Climate zones can be restrictive and they change noticeably from one place to the next. It is necessary to consider prevailing weather conditions of the site before selecting plants for planting.

7. **Soil conditions:** Some places have poor soil. Some plants don't care and others do. The one common soil deficiency that can be detrimental to plants is deep drainage. In order to check soil's drainage, dig a hole 18 inches deep and fill it with water. If water is still there 4 hours later there's a problem. In this case it's best to not choose plants that require good drainage because many plants need it. Another option is to build raised planter beds. This will accommodate smaller plants only.

D. Design Guidelines

The basics of quality landscape design apply to all projects. The following are a few of the guidelines to be employed:

1. Preserve and enhance existing natural landforms and vegetation and use regionally native plant materials as far as possible.
2. Adopt design solutions that minimize adverse impacts on the natural habitat.
3. Prevent pollution by reducing fertilizer and pesticide requirements: use integrated pest management techniques, recycle green waste and minimize runoff throughout the design process.
4. Plan low maintenance landscapes responding to energy conservation and prefer the use of water-efficient plant material.
5. Install standardized, water-efficient irrigation systems to minimize opportunities for vandalism to key components such as controllers and backflow preventers.
6. Screen incompatible elements such as chain-link fenced service, storage, utility, loading, delivery, mechanical areas and heavy traffic from view with architectural walls or dense evergreens. Use mass plantings, berms and architecturally compatible fencing as screens and buffers.
7. Combine massing of trees and shrubs with fencing and signage to create attractive and interesting entries.
8. Use thornless and non-toxic plant material near children play areas.
9. Use site amenities which are durable, well constructed and vandal-resistant.

EXERCISE

1. What are the various elements of Landscape Design composition? Explain with sketches.
2. What are the various principles of Landscape Design composition? Explain with sketches.
3. What are the major aspects of plant selection?
4. What are the basic guidelines for good Landscape Design?
5. For a site of 75m × 50m in front of an educational building, develop a Landscape Plan using fundamentals of Landscape Design composition.

4

Site Planning

While preparing a landscape design on a site, the natural resources should be identified. These include availability of solar energy, flora, fauna, water, soil, and geological formations. A natural resources inventory should be done to identify the site's environmental features. Based on this inventory, high priority resources for conservation (*e.g.,* trees, waterway, snags, and micro-habitats) should be identified. A clear plan for the conservation of those resources during each stage of site development should be prepared. The typical site analysis includes the site location and size, neighbourhood context, zoning, legal aspects, geology, physical features (natural and man-made), hydrology, soils, vegetation, wildlife, climate, culture, pedestrian and vehicular circulation, access, utilities, historic factors, density, senses stimulation, and any other factor deemed appropriate for the particular site. The aim of the plan should be to protect, restore, and improve the natural features of the site. Basically, take advantage of the good things nature has to offer and protect against the bad aspects of the site.

A. Minimize slope disturbance

1. Limit development on steep slopes (slopes greater than or equal to 25%). Leaving a slope undisturbed reduces the risk of disturbing natural hydrological drainage and causing long and short-term erosion on the site, which can pollute water sources and damage local ecology. A typical slope breakdown is given below:

   1. 0 to 2% : good for development
   2. 2 to 8% : good for most types of development
   3. 8 to 16% : restricted development
   4. 16 to 24% : not suitable for most development
   5. 24% & above : not suitable for any development

2. Complete a hydrological/soil stability study for steep slopes and use this study to guide the design of all structures onsite.

3. Align road or extended driveway with natural topography to minimize its grade and reduce cut and fill.

4. Reduce long-term erosion effects through the design and implementation of terracing, retaining walls, and stabilization techniques.

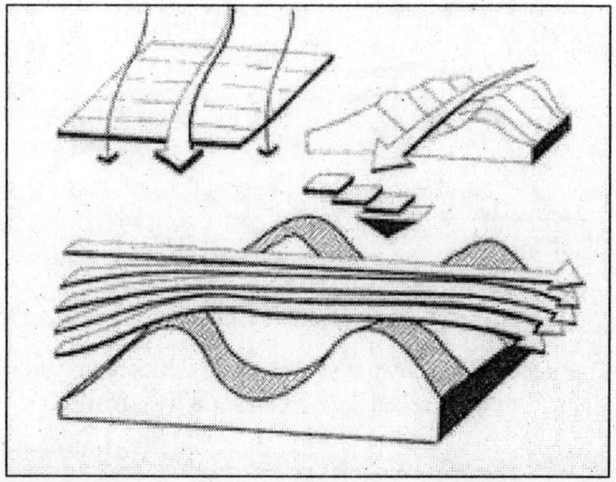

Fig. 4.1. Flat site experience little variation. Air speed increases up the slope and decrease down it. Depression valleys experience lower air temperatures. They have little air movement unless they lie in the direction of airflow.

Fig. 4.2. Pressure Difference caused by obstacles

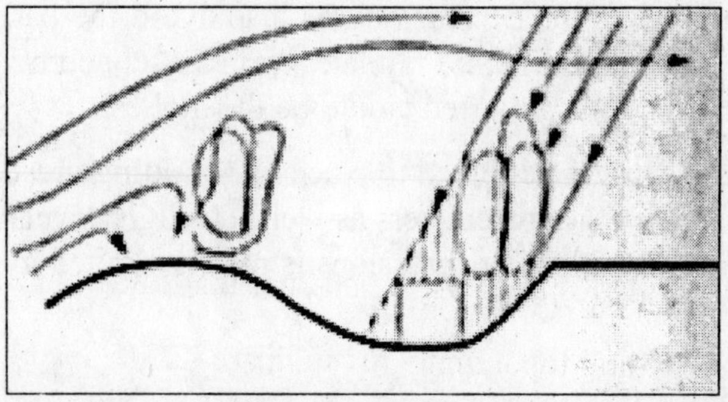

Fig. 4.3. Building in a depression and shading from heat and wind, minimizes heat gain and discomfort

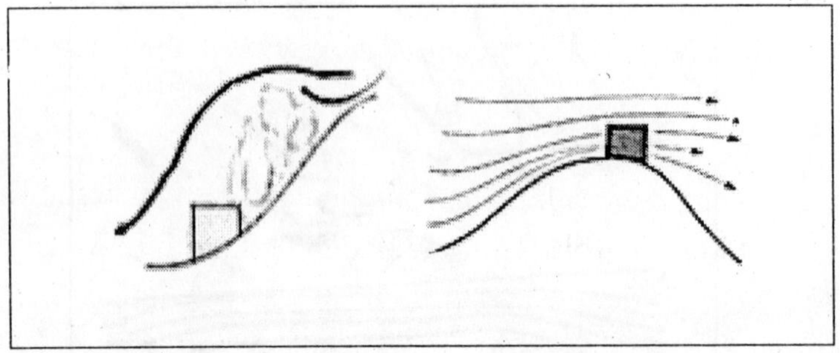

Fig. 4.4. Cool mass of air descending down a slope can be deflected or minimized by thick vegetation. Air speeds are greatest on the crest

B. Location of buildings

The landform or topography of a site and surrounding could either be flat, sloping or undulating (mounds etc.). If the land is flat, similar conditions would prevail over the entire site. The location of the building in such a case is not dictated by climatic concerns. However, slopes and depressions lead to different levels of air temperature and air movement at different parts of the site. Cooler air tends to collect in depression or dips in the land. As a result, the air temperature is lower in such areas. Also air speed increases up the windward slope. Air speed is maximum at the crest and minimum on the leeward side.

These facts can be easily understood. Cool air has a higher density than hot air. As a result cool air is heavier and tends to settle down in depressions while hot air rises. This fact also explains convection currents in liquids and gases. On the other hand, air movement is also affected by pressure difference. Airflow normally takes place from high-pressure zones to low-pressure zones. Obstacles in the path of airflow cause an air-buildup and therefore a high-pressure area on the windward side. Similarly, direction of the airflow would now depend on the shape of the obstacle and the magnitude of the pressure difference. Further, as the area through which a fluid flows decreases, fluid velocity increases and vice versa.

These facts would have an implication on the building design. In hot climates building in a depression implies relatively lower air temperatures. When building on a slope, the leeward side is preferable, as long as the orientation is acceptable. In both cases warm breezes would be minimized. The collection of water in a depression might allow for a water body. This would also be beneficial in cooling the place. In cooler climates do not place the building in the depression and also avoid the path of the cool air down the slope. Here, again, vegetation could help in protecting from cool breezes. In humid climates, primary concern is maximizing air movement. Therefore, place the building on the top of the windward slope where the air speed would be the highest.

However, even in a cold or humid climate we might be forced to place our building in a depression. If so, take measures to mitigate the effects. The placement of the building might affect other parameters as well. Daylight levels in a depression will have to be considered. In hot climates the relatively lower air temperature obtained in depressions is mostly limited to the minimum nighttime temperature. In some cases, this may be uncomfortable.

C. Minimize soil disturbance and erosion

1. Schedule construction activities to minimize time that soil is exposed. Use alternative means to install utilities, such as tunneling

instead of trenching, use of smaller equipment, shared trenches or easements, and placement of utilities under streets instead of yards.

2. Demarcate limits of clearing and grading.
3. Use fencing to protect vegetation and sensitive areas from construction vehicles, material storage and washout.
4. Install and maintain sediment and erosion controls. Use vegetation, grading, and stabilisation techniques to prevent erosion. Conserve good soil for later use.

- Consider installing retention ponds and berms to control erosion, manage storm water, and reduce heat islands while also serving as physical barriers to control access to a building and to deflect the effects of a blast.
- Use native or climate tolerant trees to improve the quality of the site as well as provide protection by obscuring assets and people.
- Implement erosion control measures to stabilize the soil (*e.g.,* seeding and mulching, installing pervious paving) and/or to retain sediment after erosion has occurred (*e.g.,* earth dikes and sediment basins). These help to reduce the negative impacts on water and air quality as well as mitigate potential damage to a building's foundation and structural system due to floods, mudslides, torrential rainstorms, and other natural hazards.

Identify a practical way to promote water quality and conserve onsite ecological habitat by reducing soil disturbance and erosion. Sediment and the pollutants contained in it are recognized sources of water quality problems. Exposed soils should be minimized to reduce erosion, promote water quality, and reduce damage caused to native vegetation. Heavy equipment and excessive digging can result in compaction or loss of topsoil along with the introduction of invasive and problematic flora. Minimizing soil disturbance and erosion reduces stress on downstream water bodies and saves valuable topsoil for the site.

D. Manage storm water using low impact development

1. Preserve and utilize natural water and drainage features.
2. Develop and implement storm water management plans that minimize concentrated flows and try to adopt natural hydrology.
3. Minimize impervious surfaces and use permeable materials for driveways, parking areas, walkways, and patios.
4. Capture storm water runoff on site, design for storm water retention features on site like pervious pavement. Use vegetated swales and depressions to reduce runoff.

Percolation through soil is one of the most effective means for filtering pollutants carried by storm water. By using natural water and drainage features, minimizing impervious surfaces, and distributing storm water flows, builders can reduce harmful pollutants carried off site while safely and effectively managing much of their storm water load onsite.

E. Prepare site plan to limit water and energy demand

1. Formulate a plan to restore or enhance natural vegetation that is cleared during development. Within this plan, phase landscaping to ensure denuded areas are quickly vegetated.
2. Limit turf areas of landscaped area, selecting native and regionally appropriate trees and vegetation in a way that complements the natural setting.

3. Group plants with similar watering needs
4. Specify planting of trees to increase site shading and moderate temperatures.
5. Design vegetative windbreaks or channels as appropriate to local conditions.
6. Onsite tree trimmings or waste of regionally appropriate trees to be used during construction as a base for walking path.
7. Establish an integrated pest management plans to minimize chemical use in pesticides and fertilizers.
8. Maximise the use of existing trees and other vegetation to shade walkways, parking lots, and other open areas. Ensure that site work and landscaping are integrated with security and safety design.
9. Take advantage of natural ventilation.
10. Maximize daylight use.
11. Investigate potential impact of future developments adjacent to the site (*e.g.,* solar, day lighting, ventilation, etc.).

Landscaping water use accounts for approximately 50% of a home's total water needs. Conservation of this valuable resource through such techniques as group plants with similar watering needs, reducing turf area, and selecting regionally appropriate plants is a key component to responsible building. Thoughtful selection and placement of plants can also reduce heating and cooling loads, provide habitat for native fauna, and minimise the heat-island effect of developments.

Water absorbs relatively large amount of radiation. They also allow evaporative cooling. As a result, during the daytime areas around water bodies are generally cooler. At night, however, water bodies release relatively large amounts of heat to the surroundings. This heat can be used for warming purposes.

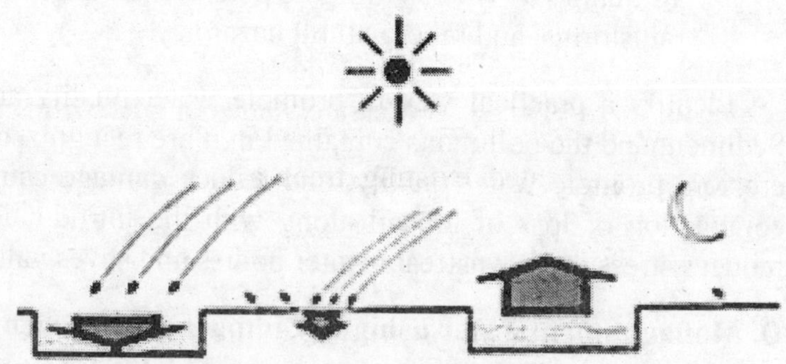

Fig. 4.5. Water bodies absorb much heat during the day and reradiate it at night

The above stated phenomena are rather easy to understand. Water has a relatively high latent heat of evaporation as well as specific heat. In other words, water uses up a comparatively large amount of heat in evaporating. It also absorbs or releases a comparatively large amount of heat for a unit rise or fall of temperature. So, when water evaporates by the movement of air, it cools the air. This is evaporative cooling. In the process humidity rises. Evaporation is slow if the relative humidity is already high. Water has a specific heat, a little more than twice that of concrete. This means that the same volume of water would absorb about twice as much heat as concrete for the same rise of temperature. This can either reduce heat gain or if desired the radiation absorbed can be used as an indirect source of heat.

In hot-dry climates, water/ water bodies can be used both for evaporative cooling as well as minimizing heat gain. Taking into account wind patterns and vegetation they can be used to direct cool breeze into the house. A roof pond minimizes heat gain through the roof. In cold climates, water bodies are beneficial only if their heat gain and loss can be controlled. This would happen only if the building can enclose the water body. However, we may be faced with a large water body in a cold region. The best thing to do then is to stay away from it. The wind pattern would have to be studied and winds avoided either by building location, vegetation pattern or both. In warm-humid regions water bodies are best avoided. The heightened humidity levels would offset the minimal benefit provided by evaporative cooling.

F. Minimize Habitat Disturbance

1. Keep land disturbance to a minimum and retain prime vegetation features to the extent possible.
2. Reduce building and paving footprints.
3. Limit site disturbance to a minimal area around the building perimeter, including locating buildings adjacent to existing infrastructure.
4. Plan construction staging areas with the environment in mind.
5. In northern climates, site parking and pedestrian areas so that they have sun exposure for assistance in melting the snow or ice.
6. Use non-toxic snow and ice removal methods.

G. Conserve existing vegetation

Minimize disturbance of and damage to trees and other vegetation designated for protection through installation of fencing and avoidance of trenching, significant changes in grade, and compaction of soil and critical root zones.

Prepare designated existing trees and vegetation for the impacts of construction through pruning, root pruning, fertilizing, and watering.

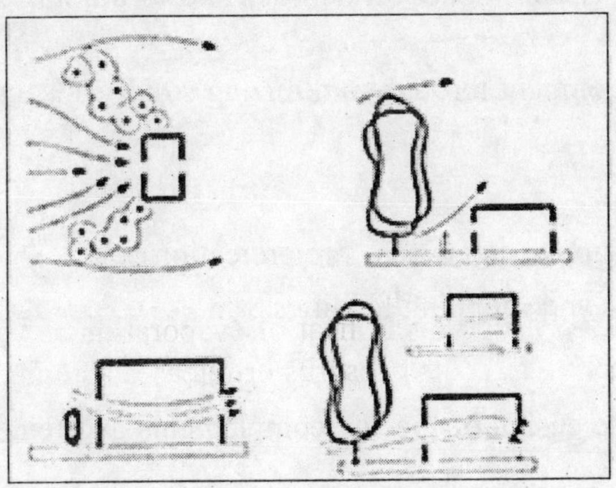

Fig. 4.6. Vegetation increasing, decreasing and directing airflow

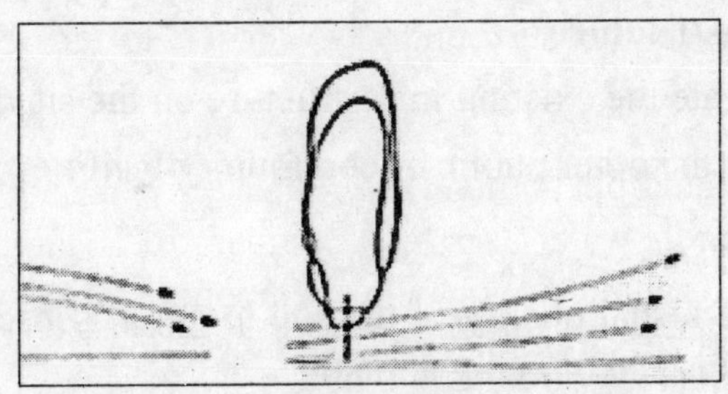

Fig. 4.7. Vegetation causes pressure differences, which shifts the air path

After identifying the existing vegetation to be conserved onsite, practical steps must be taken during the development stage to achieve the intended conservation. Such steps should include pre-development preparation of the vegetation and protection of the foliage, soil, and root system of designated vegetation.

H. Prime Parameters: Air movement, Radiation

Keeping the above in mind conduct the following analysis

1. Topographic and Soil Analysis

First, perform a slope analysis of the site showing the slopes in 4 classes: 0-5%, 5-10%, 10-15% and above 15%, to highlight the suitability of the different areas for development. Second, study the floodplain and storm water drainage patterns. These analyses can be done by using soil types and drainage analysis. Although the soil analysis will be done at the site level, but the drainage analysis should be performed for about 2-kilometer radius.

- consider building/land interface to minimize disturbance to site character, skyline, vegetation, hydrology, and soils.
- consolidate functions or segment facilities to reduce footprint of individual structures to allow sensitive placement within existing landforms.
- use landforms and the sensitive arrangement of buildings to help diminish the visual impact of facilities.

2. Vegetation analysis

- analyze the existing vegetation like woodlands, wetlands, forest, hill, stream, pasture, shoreline etc. on the site. Any other outstanding environmental features like wildlife should be evaluated.
- locate and size facilities to avoid cutting mature vegetation and to minimize disruption to, or disassociation with, other natural features
- use natural vegetation and adjustments in building plan to diminish the visual impact of facilities and to minimize imposition on environmental context
- in warmer climates, strengthen interplay of facilities with their site environment through minimizing solid walls, creating outdoor activity spaces, etc.

3. Public Infrastructure

- Investigate the existing infrastructure on the site (*i.e.,* sewer lines, water supply, electricity, fire protection);
- Identify the other public or community facilities in the area like recreation and shopping facilities.

4. Visual Analysis

Analyze the visual quality of the site to get a 'sense of the place', so that the design of the site complements and reinforces the local visual flavour, instead of being a misfit.

- enhance visual quality by creating a rhythm of open spaces and framed views. Orient visitors to building entrances
- highlight key landmarks, vistas, and facilities

Architect and Urban Planner Kevin Lynch study of the elements of urban form (edges, paths, districts, nodes and landmarks) can be used to analyze the visual context surrounding the site. Then identify the site's unique qualities, (*e.g.,* 'the views and vistas to and natural and cultural features from the site). Lynch's concept of place legibility is essentially the ease with which people understand the layout of a place. By introducing this idea, Lynch was able to isolate distinct features of a city, and see what specifically is making it so vibrant, and attractive to people. To understand the layout of a city, people first and foremost create a mental map. Mental maps of a city are mental representations of what the city contains, and its layout according to the individual.

These mental representations, along with the actual city, contain many unique elements, which are defined by Lynch as a network of paths, edges, districts, nodes, and landmarks.

1. **Paths** are channels by which people move along in their travels.
   Example: roads, paths, and sidewalks.
2. **Edges** are all other lines not included in the path group.
   Example: walls and seashores.
3. **Districts** are sections of the city, usually relatively substantial in size, which have an identifying character about them.
   Example: A wealthy neighbourhood.
4. **Nodes** are points or strategic spots where there is an extra focus, or added concentration of city features.
   Example: a busy intersection or a popular city center.
5. **Landmarks** are external physical objects that act as reference points.
   Example: a store, mountain, school, or any other object that aids in orientation when way-finding.

I. Geological and seismic data

There may be places, which are prone to earthquakes and other natural disasters. On such soils there is a need to take into account the geological and seismic data so that all precautions are taken for the construction of buildings. Determine soil substrate and potential seismic risk use shear walls and appropriate building anchorage and bracing details

- minimize excavation and disturbance to groundcover
- minimize erosion by avoiding large impervious surface areas and building footprints that collect rain and create concentrate runoff onto site.

EXERCISE

1. Explain the following with sketches with reference to site planning
   (*a*) Slope disturbance
   (*b*) Location of buildings
   (*c*) Soil disturbance and erosion
   (*d*) Low impact development
   (*e*) Water and energy demand
   (*f*) Habitat Disturbance
   (*g*) Existing vegetation
2. Explain the following with reference to site planning
   (*a*) Topographic and Soil Analysis
   (*b*) Vegetation analysis
   (*c*) Public Infrastructure
   (*d*) Visual Analysis
   (*e*) Geological and seismic data
3. Landscape designer can create a comfortable micro-climate through efficient selection and placement of plants, trees and water bodies. Explain with the help of examples.

5

Planting Design

A. Planting Design Fundamentals

The main reasons for planting design are use, ecology and aesthetics. There are number of ways of growing and combining ornamental plants. In a small garden it may be difficult to decide which plants to include. In general, fewer plants with foliage, flowers, shape, attractive bark or fruit are always better than large number of plants. Deciding on a planting design concept is useful as a basis for selecting plants. In formal planting a simple, symmetrical precisely clipped dividing hedges are provided. Formal beds using limited shapes, colors and textures are used. Framed Planting is often used in large gardens. The idea is to create a clearly defined framework using fences, hedges or walls. The term 'framed planting' describes the use of a background to enhance a special feature, specimen shrub or tree, plant group or a distant view. Free planting offers natural and free-flowing style than framed or formal schemes. It combines a wide range of plants in an attractive and informal way. These gardens are usually difficult to manage because of wide-ranging collections of plants.

Plants are the essence of a garden. Plants are the living beings in nature. Plants are dynamic life forms: flowering, fruiting, reproducing, maturing and eventually dying. The ultimate goal of combining plants in the garden is to achieve harmony. Plants should harmonize with the unique qualities of the site, buildings and materials, and other plants in a way that complement each other. Plant characteristics must be taken into account in making a planting plan. Major characteristics are: form, color, texture, time of bloom, species of plant and cultural needs. Thus there could be spring gardens, rose gardens, alpine gardens or old-fashioned gardens.

The planting methods and the functions intended to serve in designed landscapes have been expanding. While serving as sources of aesthetic pleasure, plants also reinforce the existing native ecosystem and work as bioengineering agents for soil retention and restoration. Efforts should be made to support the existing visual character and ecological function of the site within its regional context wherever it is feasible. The use of native plants mixed with a small proportion of compatible exotics adds interest and variety.

The microclimate of an outdoor space can be changed through careful planting of trees and shrubs to block excessive sun or wind. Plantings can also reduce snow drifting across roads. Plant screens can provide privacy, indicate boundaries, discourage trespassers or block unpleasant views. Plantings can control and direct the movements of people, animals or vehicles. Plants are harvested for food, flowers and raw building materials. They also provide food and shelter for wildlife. Planting encourages the presence of birds, butterflies or other forms of wildlife.

B. The Design Roles of Plants

Site inventory, analysis and conceptual designs for circulation and hardscape materials (patios, walkways, benches, fountains) should be completed before the planting design can begin. Each plant species has its own characteristics. Every plant variety has a certain mature height, spread, form and ornamental qualities. A thorough understanding of the plant's character should be known before planting design. For defining spaces in a planting design, plants can be categorized by height as canopy trees (greater than 60′), tall trees (40'-60'), short trees (20'-40'), large shrubs (15'-20'), medium shrubs (8'-15'), small shrubs (4'-6'), mini-shrubs and groundcovers (6"-4') and herbaceous plants (plants that die back completely to the ground each winter). When beginning a planting design, it is best to start with plants such as trees and shrubs with permanent stems.

In planting design choose those shapes, colors, and textures which already naturally exist. In many landscape designs individual plants are necessarily the essential elements of the composition. Plants are living things. They grow from year to year to the height of their development and die. They change their appearance with the seasons. Consider the changes in the appearance of plants during their whole growth as well as their cycle of seasonal changes. Plants texture, symmetry and shape will stay for a long time under good maintenance or quickly lost without it. Design often depends on the degree of maintenance that can be expected.

The forms, colors and textures offered by plants give to the designer certain opportunities and also certain limitations. Understanding the characteristics of plant material is an essential skill of landscape design.

C. Plant Forms

Form is an important aesthetic criterion for species selection. The form of a plant is its three-dimensional shape. It can be seen from various directions and distances. These different viewpoints and scales affect our comprehension of the form. There is a great variety in the forms of trees and shrubs and herbaceous plants. It is possible to describe major types although plant form is varied. Each of these can have a particular role in planting composition. A plant inherited form can be affected by environmental factors. The forms are similar only in the growth of the individual plant. They are all symmetrical on a central axis. Due to physical necessities of their growth, all plants are balanced forms. Almost any free-standing plant, not distorted by some unusual influence is an individual and self-sufficient object in the composition. The use of forms in composition applies equally to all kinds of plants except with herbaceous plants and shrubs. Their interest lies in their flower. They are more often planted in masses where individual shape is not important.

Each species of tree tends to have its different forms in youth, maturity and old age. All trees are influenced in their form by nourishment in the soil, the shade and the wind. All forms of trees are made by their subordinate parts like branches and sprays in relation to the trunk.

D. Plant Texture

Plant texture is the visual roughness or smoothness of any part of the plant. A plant is commonly referred to as having coarse, fine or medium texture. Texture, like form, depends on viewing distance. The texture of a plant is the result of the shape, size and surface of the leaves. Large leaves give a plant a coarse texture and certain strength of appearance. Small leaves give a plant a certain haziness of outline and an effect of softness and delicacy. This scale relation of texture is very important in planting design. If the landscape designer plants a long straight avenue with individual trees of twenty feet in diameter and thirty feet apart, the effect of the row of trees might be a straight line. However, if the same designer plants a flower bed edging in a straight line of five feet length, then one would be compelled to use such things as box bushes, not more than six inches in diameter.

Fig. 5.1. Different plant forms

Texture may provide the aesthetic theme for composition but care is needed with the balance of harmony and contrast. Bold texture can provide an exciting theme in a large space. Use of bold textures is common with modern buildings. This is sometimes called 'architectural planting'. The use of fine textures is common in historic landscapes. A plantation may be unified by plants of similar texture, also planted areas may be differentiated by texture of its plants. Similarly a bed in a garden may be unified and diversified by a judicious choice of textures.

Fig. 5.2. Different plant textures

E. Plant Color

Color is the essence of the garden. Many beautiful garden and landscape plantings are created by restricting colors of flowers, fruits, stems and foliage to a limited range. The success of restricted color themes is that a degree of variety and contrast will be provided by the colors of plant foliage. Good color combinations and coordination can have a dramatic impact in garden design, so choosing plants that complement or contrast with each other is essential. Gray (silvers), blacks and whites are considered neutral colors. These colors are best used in the background with bright colors in the foreground. They can also be used successfully in many color combinations. Plant selection could include silver and reds, silver and purples, silver and yellows, or any number of combinations.

A plant with many leaves close together appears to be almost of one uniform color. A plant with open foliage has the general color of its leaves dotted with dark points of shadow. In a tree with thick and heavy leaves, the interior shadow is dark; whereas a tree with thin and semitransparent leaves, the inner part of the mass may be full of green light.

There is a great variety within the range of green color of foliage. In addition to this, the trees and shrubs with foliage of another color than green give striking appearance. Within the range of greens, the designer can create many effects. Dark colors give a plant a certain effect of solidity and weight. The dark colors tend to give an effect of soberness, whereas light colors give certain amount of gaiety. A judicious contrast of dark green against light green will enhance the effect of both colors and differentiate the foliage. In large-scale design, color may be used within reasonable limits to enhance the effects of aerial perspective.

Where there is no necessity for similarity with the natural foliage of the region, red and yellow colored foliage may be desirable. These brilliant colors give value and effect against more usual and restful shades. The color possibilities of deciduous plants are not at an end when their foliage is gone. There are many rich textures of gray, brown and purple. Their value lies largely in their contrast with their surroundings. It is possible to spoil this effect by too wide-spread planting of such material.

The landscape designer has his greatest opportunity in the use of color in flowering shrubs and particularly in flowering herbaceous plants. In these plants there is a wide range of color to experiment. The landscape designer cannot look at the colors before he puts them into picture like a painter. The plants should be brought from a nursery or raised from seed with no guide to know their color except the general knowledge of what color of flower a certain plant should bear. There are various color schemes but no scheme has attained general acceptance. The plants in a garden are bathed in sun or overlaid with shade, and so their colors may be overlapping one another. The color masses of the flowers are not contiguous. Their color is diluted by masses of foliage and by patches of darkness. White flowers are harmonious with flowers of any other color. The designer may avoid doubtful combinations by interposing white flowers between the masses of possibly inconsistent color. Where flower colors are intended to be seen from a long distance, color contrasts may be effective. In a landscape composition, the large relation of each mass of flower to the whole scene must be remembered. It is possible to clarify and accent the whole design of a garden by a proper choice of the flower colors of the beds.

F. Plant Character

The character of an individual plant is the result of two factors: its species and the soil & moisture conditions, Plants are recognized as different in species having certain characteristics like the growth of the trunk, the arrangement of branches, the grouping of its branches and leaves. Any individual species is known for this typical shape. The character of an individual plant is the result of its species and environment. Plants from the same environment are often similar in appearance. Plants found in the same environment are likely to go well together as elements in planting design. To reproduce the character of some native piece of landscape, it is better to confine planting to native plant materials.

The plants used in a landscape composition must be considered by the designer in different aspects whether they form a wall or screen or edging. The separating wall between one open area and another in a scheme will usually be formed largely of tree masses. Where these tree masses form the boundary of an irregular open space, their compositional relations may be more complicated. The principles of repetition, sequence and balance are still to be considered in an informal way.

A hedge is a foliage wall. A hedge may be very rough in texture or it may be carefully decorated. The plants forming hedges expose their own character to the resulting structure. A formal row of plants spaced some distance apart may be effective as a screen. When hedges are low enough, they define the boundary between two masses within the same view. Both masses being visible at the same time, both forms must be studied in the composition.

Fig 5.3 Typical Hedge Planting

Fig 5.4 Typical Garden borders

G. Specimen Trees and Shrubs

A single foliage mass must have unity and individuality to make it worthy of composition. Such individuality is usually expressed by an individual plant, tree, shrub or flowering plant. Striking color may serve this purpose. Shape is most important characteristic which give individuality to plants. A "specimen" tree or shrub may be worthy of a dominant position like the centuries-old flowering cherry tree in the court of a Japanese temple.

Fig. 5.5. Typical Specimen trees & shrubs

The interest and value which a group of trees or shrubs may have depend largely on the composition. The main form of the group may be decided by its relation to the whole scene: it may be rounded or bending according to the purpose it serves in the total composition. The composition of any group of plants will depend on the point from where it is seen. The designer mostly deals in groups of three or more trees or shrubs. A good group of three will have one tree dominant and two subordinate by means of shape, color or texture.

Fig. 5.6. Typical Conifers specimen trees shrubs

Fig. 5.6. Typical plant arrangement

H. Arrangement of plants in relation to color

Primary importance of herbaceous plants lies in their flowers. Attractive flowers enable them to give a dominant interest to the recess in which they are set. A flower bed in a garden should have a boundary by edgings of stone or brick or concrete. Often the boundary line of the bed is marked by some kind of plant edging. Plan for a succession of plants in bloom to have the bed interesting at all times. This is possible in two ways: plant perennials throughout in such a way that one kind of flower after another comes into bloom or remove certain plants when they are through blooming and replace them. The flowering plants are normally arranged in a formal bed to make harmonious pattern in color and properly related to the shape of the bed. Different plants come to their full height at different times and bloom at different times. The same bed will present a sequence of different patterns during the season.

I. Tree Planting

Tree planting can be used for screening, separating, sheltering and enclosing landscape surroundings. For design purposes trees can be divided into small: mature height 5–10 meters; medium: 10–20 meters; and tall: above 20 meters.

Small trees of similar height are mainly local to the spaces between buildings. Medium trees can create spaces having greater effect on the spatial structure of the landscape. Tall trees are less common in urban areas because of the space they demand. The size of trees over 20 meters enables them to form the part of the primary spatial structure of streets, squares and parks. In the rural landscape large trees create a large-scale framework.

Medium and tall tree planting can play a crucial role in integrating big buildings into the surrounding landscape. Tree belts and plantations provide screening of near distance views. The ability of trees to screen views than shrub planting can be made use of to manipulate views as the observer moves through the landscape. Carefully located gaps in planting open up vistas or frame a focus. A frame of branches or foliage directs attention and focuses the mind.

A single specimen or small group of trees acts as a focus. A tree with a distinctive feature such as color will make a notable focus. Large tree specimens or groups have this effect at some distance. When single specimens or small groups of trees accompany buildings, the relationship between the form of the tree and the building can be interesting. A simple, regular line of one species can bind together different building styles.

Fig 5.7. Typical Avenue tree planting

Fig 5.8. Typical Coniferous-trees

Fig 5.9. Typical Deciduous-trees

Trees can enhance aesthetic quality, provide visual and wind screening, solar access and habitat for wildlife, and also acts as shelter-belts and amenity in recreational and open space areas. The following should be considered when designing for trees

1. Selection of an appropriate species for its intended purpose.
2. The mature height and crown spread of the tree.
3. The tree spacing in different types of tree planting.
4. Clearances from above and below ground services, as well as new and proposed buildings.
5. Allow 10 metres for large trees and 6 metres for medium trees for canopy development. Allow 3 metres for screens, shelterbelts or park group planting.
6. Sight lines for both pedestrian, cycle and vehicular traffic.

Trees often do not grow properly when planted in areas with impervious surfaces due to lack of water and air. Providing more space around the tree should reduce these problems. The following trees are commonly seen in India

1. **Aloe Vera:** Aloe Vera grows to a height of 12 to 16 inches. It has a fibrous root system. It does not have stems. It has thick fresh leaves with sharp points, which are up to 18 inches long and 2 inches wide at the base. Its leaves are even long and triangular in shape. The tissue in the center of the Aloe leaf contains a gel, which yields the aloe gel. Its leaves are rich in water to survive for years. These leaves have spiky margins and are blotched creams. It is the member of the Lilly family. The roots of the plant are

thick and fibrous. The fruit is the triangular capsule containing numerous seeds. Aloe Vera is cultivated throughout India. It mainly grows in the tropical and sub tropical areas. It grows well on sandy and well-drained soil. Aloe Vera plant is spread through the seed. It prefers a well-drained sandy soil in sunny location. Aloe Vera needs the temperature of above 40° degrees. They should be potted in the spring season and watered carefully. It grows in the arid climate. They should be watered regularly in the summers, but over watering can kill the plant. It also grows in partial shade. It reaches the maturity in four years when the leaves are harvested. Aloe Vera is a very popular potted plant. It is grown in houses for the decoration. The leaf sap is used to make a soothing and healing moisturizing cream, which is good for the dry skin. It is used in the making of anti wrinkle cream. It is even used in the preparation of shampoos.

Fig. 5.10. Aloe Vera

Fig. 5.11. Amla

2. **Amla:** Amla is the medium size deciduous plant. It grows to the height of 8-18 meters. It has a crooked trunk and spreading branches. Its flower is yellow greenish in color. The fruit is spherical pale yellow with six vertical lines. The mature fruits are hard and do not fall for the gentle touch. The average weight of the fruit is 60 -70 gms. It has a grey bark and reddish wood. Its leaves are feathery, linear oblong in shape and smell like lemon. Its wood is hard in texture. It wraps and splits when exposed in the Sun or in the excessive heat. It is planted in tropical India and on the hill slopes up to 2000 meter. Amla can grow in light and heavy soils. It is grown under the tropical conditions. The young plants are protected from the hot winds as they die easily. Amla is generally spread through seeds. It requires proper sunlight. It is irrigated during the monsoon season. It starts bearing fruits in seven years from the day of planting. It is the main ingredient used in the shampoo. Amla is used in sauces, candy, dried chips, pickle, jellies and powder. It is even used in the dyeing industry. Its extract is popularly used in the ink. Amla wood is commonly used in firework.

3. **Arjuna tree:** Arjuna is a large size deciduous tree. The height of the Arjuna tree reaches up to 60-85 feet. It is an evergreen tree with the yellow flowers and conical leaves. It has a smooth grey bark. Its fruit is 2.5 -3.5 cm long, fibrous woody, glabrous with 5

hard wings, striated with numerous curved veins. It has a buttressed trunk and a vast spreading crown from which the branches drop downwards. Its leaves are dull green above and pale brown beloco. Arjuna flowers between March to June and fruits between September to November. Terminalia Arjuna is common throughout India. Its fruit is dried in the sunlight and then stored up to 6-12 months. Seeds are pre-treated by soaking in the water for 48 hours before sowing in beds. Seedlings 8–9 months are better to transplant in the field. Its wood is used in boat and house building because it is very hard. Its wood is also used in the making of the agricultural implements and weapons. It is grown in the cities and towns for the purpose of shade.

Fig. 5.12. Arjuna tree

Fig. 5.13. Ashwagandha

4. **Ashwagandha:** Ashwagandha is an evergreen shrub that grows up to the height of 0.5 m to 1.5 m. It is covered by the leaves all round the year. The flowers are hermaphrodite (they have both the male and the female organs) and are greenish yellow in color. Its fruit and berries are orange-red in colour. Its roots are whitish brown in color. Aswagandha is a small woody shrub and flowers throughout the year. Ashwagandha is grown in all parts of India. It is found in the woodland garden, cultivated beds and dappled shade. Ripe red fruits of the plant are dried in the warm and well-ventilated space. After some days the berries are separated, washed and dried up properly. Its seed can be shown in the early spring. They get germinated within two weeks in light sandy, medium loamy and well-drained soil. It grows more in the sunlight than in the shade. Ashwagandha is used as the substitute of the soaps. The leaves are an insect repellent. Aswagandha mixed with the almond oil and rose water is used as the facial toner.

5. **Banyan tree:** Banyan tree is a huge tree with very extensive branches. It is an evergreen tree. Its branches spread out and send trunk like roots to the ground to support itself. It grows to a height of more than 21 meters and lives for many years. The leaves are 10-20 cm long with many aerial roots. The leaves are broad, oval and glossy. It can grow into a giant tree covering several hectares. It is found in almost all the parts of India. In India its edible leaves are used as the plates. It is planted for the soil conservation. Wood is used for well curbs, door panels, boxes, furniture etc. It is suitable for paper pulp. The wood of the aerial roots is stronger and is used for the tent poles and cart yokes.

Fig. 5.14. Banyan tree

Fig. 5:15. Brahmi

6. **Brahmi:** Brahmi is the small creeping herb with numerous branches. It grows to a height of 2-3 feet and its branches are 10-35 cm long. It has oval shaped leaves that are 1-2 cm long and 3-8 mm wide. Leaves are formed in pairs along the stems. Small-tubular, five petal flowers are white- purple in color. Its stem is soft, juicy and hairy with the glands. Roots emerge out of the nodules and directly go to the soil. The fruit is oval and sharp at apex. Brahmi is found in marshy areas near streams and ponds throughout India especially in the North eastern regions. It is found at elevations from sea level to altitudes of 4,400 feet. Brahmi is spread by seed, cuttings and also by the root division. Before establishing the plant cutting, the field should be ploughed properly and made free of weeds. The cuttings should be 4-5 cm long containing roots and leaves. Hand weeding is required every 5-20 days. It grows faster in the high temperature (33-42 Degree Celsius) and humidity (65-80%). It prefers wet spots. It is grown in the pots in the house garden. It can grow in both the sun and shade. It requires water from time to time because its roots are shallow. It also requires regular organic fertilizer for its growth. It gives flowers and fruit in the summer season. It requires moderate to high lightening to grow well. Brahmi is rich in Vitamin C and can be used in the salads, soups and sandwiches. Brahmi oil restores and preserves the memory.

7. **Cork tree:** It is a tall deciduous tree. It grows up to 25 meter. The leaves are innately compound. Flowers are long tubular, white and fragrant. The fruit is a capsule. It flowers at night and shed flowers early in the morning. It has corky bark. It has straight trunk and has few branches. Cork tree widely grows in the Central India. It is mostly found in the tropical forests. Cork tree can grow in variety of soils. It requires full sunlight for its growth. Its flowers are used in the rituals. Its bark is used to produce yellow dye.

8. **Eucalyptus:** Eucalyptus is a tall evergreen tree. It attains the height of more than 300 feet. Leaves of the tree on young branches are opposite, sessile, cordate-ovate and covered with a bluish white bloom. The adult leaves are alternate and 6-12 inches long and 1-2 inches wide. Its flowers are cream in color. The appearance of its bark varies with the age of the tree. Its bark consists of long fibers and can be pulled off in long pieces. Stems of the seedlings and wood branches are quadrangular. Flowers are in cymose panicles. The fruit is a capsule. It grows well in deep, fertile, well drained loamy soil with adequate moisture. Eucalyptus grows in

well-drained sandy soil. It is spread through seeds, soft wood cuttings and semi hard wood cuttings. It must be taken into account that its roots are not broken at the time of planting. It needs water before and after planting. It requires full sunlight. Eucalyptus is used as the pulpwood in the manufacture of the paper as well as raw material. It is used as the poles for the construction of huts and houses. It is used in making plywood, doors and windows

Fig. 5.16. Cork tree

Fig. 5.17. Eucalyptus

9. **Garden Asparagus:** Garden Asparagus grows to a height of 3 feet. It is an herbaceous perennial plant. It is well known for its edible young branches. It has fleshy roots and fern-like feathery foliage. Its roots grow 3 feet down in the soil. Young branches are green juicy and tender. It has smooth and green stems, which are 4-6 feet tall. It has green slender branches, which appear more like the leaves than the branches. It produces male and female flowers on the separate plants. Flowers are greenish, bell shaped, which grows in the group of 1 to 3. Round bright red berries are produced on the female plants and each berry contains several black seeds. Garden Asparagus is found especially in the Northern India. It is widely grown in the jungles. It is mainly grown in the gardens. It is mostly spread through seed, which are allowed to grow for a year. It is mostly planted in the spring season. The plant prefers acid, neutral, and alkaline soil. It grows in semi shade or no shade. It is placed in the trench which is 12 -18 inches wide and six inches deep. It requires water regularly when it is young. Young branches come out in early spring. There are so many vegetable recipes made out the Garden Asparagus. They are normally boiled or steamed. Its young branches are taken as the raw salad.

10. **Indian Mahogany:** Indian Mahogany grows up to the height of 30 -40 feet. It is fast straight growing tree with a broad rounded symmetrical crown. It is 20 -30 feet in spread. The fruit is a large greenish brown capsule, splitting into 5 parts releasing flat, long winged, light brown seeds. Its wood is red brown in color. Both the male and the female flowers are produced on the same plant. The bark is smooth dark brown in color. The leaves are pinnate which are 12 -25 cm long, with four to eight leaflets. Indian Mahogany is found in almost all the parts of India. Indian Mahogany is mostly spread through seeds. It requires partial shade or

full Sun for its growth. It needs water periodically. It loses its leaves at the end of the winter. The new leaves start growing after two or three weeks. The new leaves are reddish purple in color, which turn yellow green later. Its wood is used in making furniture, fixtures, musical instruments, inlay, boat, caskets and many more. Its wood is a very popular material for drum making.

Fig. 5.18. Garden Asparagus

Fig. 5.19. Indian Mahogany

11. **Indian Rosewood:** Indian Rosewwod is an erect deciduous tree. It grows to the height of 25 meter and 2-3 meter in diameter. It has leathery leaves, which are up to 15 cm long. The flowers are whitish pink in color. Its crown is oval in shape. The fruit is brown and pod like in shape. The fruit is dry and hard. The sapwood is white to pale brown in color and the heartwood is golden to dark brown in color. Indian Rosewood mainly grows on the banks of the river below 900-meter elevation. Indian Rosewood is mostly propagated through the root suckers and seeds. It requires fertile well-drained soil. Seeds are soaked in water for 48 hours before sowing. Seeds are germinated in three weeks. Young Rosewood needs full sunlight. It requires dry to wet soil. Young plants are well watered until established. Flowers occur from October to February. It is the important fuel wood and is also used for shade and shelter. Its wood is used for making furniture, doors, windows, ship floors, plywood, skis, musical instruments, carvings etc. Rosewood is often used in the martial art weaponry, particulary as the shaft of spears and in the gun staves because of durability. Its oil is used in Perfumes.

12. **Indian Tulip:** Indian Tulip Tree attains the height of 40 feet or more. It is a very large tree. It has heart shaped leaves and the cup shaped flowers. It is a fast growing, evergreen tree. It is very bushy when it is young but thins out with the age. Each flower is white – yellow in color and has maroon eye that ages to purple. The flower bloom year round and lasts for three days. The major branches of the tree grow straight, with the thick corrugated bark. Its fruit is the round capsule, which is about one inch across. Its seeds are greyish brown in color. Indian Tulip tree is found in deep, rich, well-drained soils of forest coves and lower mountain slopes. Indian Tulip trees are easily spread through the seeds. It requires a deep rich soil for its cultivation. It must be taken care that the inner part of the seed is not destroyed. The seeds are germinated within 14-28 days. Tulip plant can also spread with the

cuttings. It is also grown in the pots. It sheds its leaves in the month of February. New leaves appear in the month of April and March. The fruits, flowers and young leaves are edible. The tough fibrous bark is made into rope in several areas. The bark is also used to caulk boat. Even the cork is made from the inner bark. The yellow dye is obtained from its fruits and flowers and the red one from the bark. Its parts are also used in the making of gum, oil and tannin. Its timber is also used to make the papers. Its wood is used to make bowls, paddles and other carved objects.

Fig. 5.20. Indian Rosewood

Fig. 5.21. Indian Tulip

13. **Khair tree:** It is the moderate size deciduous tree. It has rough bark which is dark gray brown in color. It grows up to the height of 15 meter. The leave are 8 -10 cm long. It has short curved spines and rough grayish brown bark. The flowers are pale yellow in color. They start appearing in the month of June -August. Fruits ripen in January to March and remain in the tree for long. The young parts are dark brown to purple in color. The tree has rough texture from outside. It grows throughout India. It is mainly spread through the stumps or seeds. The seeds are mostly sown in the month of June. It is planted on sandy and black cotton soil. The seeds germinate in the monsoons. Khair should be sown on mounds at least 61 to 76 cm in height so that the seedlings do not remain submerged in water for a long period. Irrigation is necessary for the plant. Cuttings should be made from the well developed seedlings. The root and branch should be 23-31 cm and 2.5 to 5.0 cm respectively. The wood extracts are used for tanning and dying Khaki. Its wood is used as the raw material in the raw industry. Its wood is used in ship building. The wood of Khair is used in making the plough and the pounding log for rice.

14. **Kikar:** Kikar is the small thorny tree. It grows to the height of 7-12 meter. It has yellow round head flowers which are nectar less. The bark is red-brown to blackish and rough. The leaves are light green and fern like up to 120 mm long and 50 mm wide. Flowers are 10-15 mm in diameter, which grow in cluster between 4-6 and are sweetly scented. It is mainly grown in the cold temperature. It can be grown in any type of soil. It requires water for seed germination. The bark and seeds are the source of tannin. The various parts of Kikar are useful in Diarrhoea. The leaves and the bark are useful in arresting secretion or bleeding. The gum dispels any

irritation of the skin and soothes the inflamed membranes. Fresh pods of babul tree are effective in sexual disorders like spermatorrhoea, frequent night discharges, loss of viscidity of the semen and premature ejaculation.

Fig. 5.22. Khair tree

Fig. 5.23. Kikar tree

15. Neem tree: It is a tall evergreen tree with small bright green leaves. It is up to 100 feet tall. It blossoms in spring with the small white flowers. It has a straight trunk. Its bark is hard rough and scaly and fissured. The color of the bark is brown grayish. The leaves are alternate and consist of several leaflets with saw-like edges. Its flowers are small and white in color. Neem tree is found

Fig. 5.24. Neem tree

Fig. 5.25. Peepal tree

throughout India. It is a popular village tree. Neem tree can easily grow in dry, stony, shallow and clayey soils. It needs very little water and plenty of sunlight. It grows slowly during the first year. It can be spread through the seeds and cuttings. Young Neem tree cannot tolerate excessive cold. People in India use its twigs to brush their teeth. Neem is considered as the useful tree in rehabilitating the wasteland areas. Neem seed pulp is useful for methane gas production. Neem bark is used in tanning and dyeing. Neem cake is widely used in India as fertilizer for sugarcane, vegetable and other cash crops. Many countries have been consistently growing the Neem tree against the global warming.

16. **Peepal tree:** Peepal is a large, fast growing deciduous tree. It has a heart shaped leaves. It is a medium size tree. It has a large crown with wide spreading branches. It sheds leaves in the month of March and April. The fruits of the Peepal are hidden with the figs. The figs ripen in the month of May. The figs containing the flowers grow in pairs just below the leaves. They look like the berries. Its bark is light gray and peels in patches. Its fruit is purple in color. It is one of the longest living trees. Peepal tree is grown throughout India. Peepal tree is easily spread through the seeds or through the cuttings. It can grow in any type of soil. Young peepal needs proper nourishment. It requires full sunlight and proper watering. From the bark of the Peepal tree reddish dye is extracted. Its leaves are used to feed the camels and the elephants. When the leaves are dried they are used for the decoration purpose.

Fig. 5.26. Sal

Fig. 5.27. Teak

17. **Sal:** Sal is a large sub-deciduous tree. It is up to 30 meter high. Sal tree is rarely completely leafless. It has large leathery leaves and yellowish flowers. They have tough texture. Young trees have a linear crown, which becomes rounder and flatter with aging. The sapwood is whitish in color, thick and is less durable. The heartwood becomes dark brown to black in color on exposure. The wood pores are filled with resin. Sal tree requires well-drained, moist and sandy loam soil. It can grow in any type of temperature. It is mostly spread through cuttings. In dry conditions it sheds leaves from February to March. New leaves appear in the month of April and May. The flowers mature into fruit in summers and the seeds ripen in June-July. The leaves of the Sal tree are used by

the tribal people for preparing rice cakes and for smoking. The leaves are used to make platters, bowls, small baskets and many more. Distilled leaves produce oil which is used in perfumery. It is also used in flavoring chewing gums and tobacco. Its dried and fallen leaves are used as fertilizers. It is used for caulking ships and boats. The oil coming out from its seed is edible known as Sal butter. It is often used in cooking and for the burning in the oil lamps. The seeds of the Sal tree are used for fat extraction. Its oil is even used for adulterating ghee. Tribal people give marriage invitation in the form of folded Sal leaves, with the little bit of turmeric and rice inside it.

18. **Teak:** Teak is tall evergreen tree. It has yellowish blonde to reddish brown wood. It attains the height of about 30 meter. The fruit is a drupe. It has bluish to white flowers. It produces the large leaf similar to the tobacco leaf. The bark is whitish gray in color. It generally grows straight with the uneven texture, medium lusture and the oily feel. The upper surface of the tree is rough to touch and the inner surface has hairs. The fruit is enclosed by the bladder like calyx, which is light brown, ribbed and papery. Teak is well grown in all the parts of India. The new plants can spread from cuttings. It is usually planted when they are four to six weeks old. Plough the land thoroughly and level it. The best season to plant the teak is monsoon. Carry out weeding operations regularly. Teak requires loamy soil rich in humus and having the right content of moisture with good drainage. It grows well in hilly and dry areas. It requires a dry tropical climate for its growth. It flowers in February and March. It is used in the furniture making, boat decks and for indoor flooring. It is widely used to make the doors and windows. It is resistant to the attack of termites. Its wood contains scented oil, which is the repellent to insects. The leaves yield the dye which is used to color the clothes and edible. Teak is probably the best-protected commercial species in the world.

Fig. 5.28. Tulsi

Fig. 5.29. Turmeric

19. **Tulsi:** Tulsi is heavy branched having all over hair. It attains the height of about 75-90 cm. It has round oval shaped leaves up to 5 cm long. The leaves are 2-4 cm in length. Its seeds are flat. Its flowers are purple–cream in color. The Tulsa with the green leaves is called the Shri Tulsi and one with the reddish leaves is called the Krishna Tulsi. Its seeds are yellow to reddish in color. A leaf of

Tulsi contains essential oil. Tulsi grows wild in tropics and warm regions. Tulsi seeds germinate easily. The seeds are mainly sown in the spring season. They are watered from time to time and germinated in one to two weeks. Tulsi prefers rich soil for its growth. It requires full sunlight. It is mainly grown in the temperate climate. There are several handicraft jewellery items made of Tulsi wood.

20. **Turmeric:** The plant of Turmeric is an herbaceous perennial, which is 60 -90 cm high. It has a short stem. It has large rectangular leaves and up to one meter long. Flowers of the turmeric appear on a spike like the stalk. Its flowers are yellow white in color. They are sterile and do not produce viable seed. The lamina is green above and pale green below, and is 30-40 cm long and 8-12 cm wide. Approximately 30 flowers are produced in a spike. Inflorescence is a central spike of 10-15 cm in length. Its plant looks like the ginger plant. It is the widely cultivated tropical plant of India. Turmeric is planted in the month of September to October. It grows in light black, black clayey loams, and red soils in irrigated and rain-fed conditions. The rhizomes are planted 5-7 cm deep. This crop is planted by the small rhizomes with one or two buds. It is harvested after 9-10 months of planting. The lower leaves turn yellow and fall with age. The powered rhizome of this plant is used as a condiment and as a yellow dye. It is used to color and flavor the foodstuff. It is used in the preparation of medicinal oils, ointments and poultice. It is even used in the cosmetics.

J. Plant Selection

Proper plant selection is important for successful landscaping. Plants and colors bring garden to life. They are also elements that can be used with purpose such as screening, shade, erosion control, dividing, focal points, noise control, etc. So choosing the right plants for the right place and purpose is helpful for good landscaping.

The most reliable method is to make fine distinctions between groups of plants on the basis of design characteristics. These design characteristics can be classified as functional and spatial, visual and other sensory, plant growth habit and cultural requirements.

1. **Functional and spatial:** The functional and spatial characteristics allow a plant to perform its working role in the landscape. Form and foliage density affect its ability to shelter, screen or shade. Rooting habit determines its ability to bind the surface soil and protect against erosion. Height affects its barrier function. These characteristics allow planting to produce a functioning landscape.
2. **Visual and other sensory:** Visual qualities are key ingredients in planting designed for sensory interest. It depends on the nature of the site and the visual sensitivity of the location. Lot of time and effort can be spent on detailed composition and expression for a private garden; but for a reclamation site, growing any type of plants would be the main challenge.
3. **Plant growth habit and cultural requirements:** Growth habit and cultural requirements determine whether a species can succeed in a habitat. On sites with polluted substrata, plant survival is important than the visual qualities when selecting species. Knowledge of a plant habit and horticultural preferences is essential to create sustainable planting. Unfortunately this information is not readily available in literature on landscape use of plants. Plants in landscape projects are under greater stress than those in gardens. Personal knowledge of species tolerance is very useful for the landscape designer.

A systematic plant selection method is first to establish planting function and spatial form. Then visual character and other detailed aesthetic qualities can be decided. Species and cultivars well suited to the site conditions can be chosen to perform those roles later.

Primary considerations for selecting landscape plants are:

1. Height and Width are figured by the mature size a plant will reach in both upward and outward directions. Not calculating this can

cause serious problems in the future.

2. Form is the shape of the plant and how it will occupy and accent space. Form and shape are considered as columnar, round, vase, weeping, oval, creeping, etc.
3. Texture is the fineness or roughness of plants. It can also be categorized in terms of leaf thickness and shade (light or dark) of plants. As a rule, plants with finer textures should be used in greater numbers than plants with coarse textures.
4. Seasonal interest and color are figured by the special features a plant has at different times of the year. Foliage, fruit, flowers, winter color, changing colors, etc.

Secondary considerations for selecting landscaping plants:

1. Insect and disease resistance
2. Sun or Shade
3. Moisture tolerance
4. Drought Resistance
5. Soil Type

K. Plant selection for best design and effect

A few well-selected plant varieties can have more impact and appeal than a mix match selection of one of these here and one of those there. Unity is achieved in garden design by consistency. Planting in groups of 3's, 5's, 7's, etc. also gives a sense of intentional design, balance, and unity. Growing a group of the same plants gives a stronger impact when viewed from a distance. This is true especially with perennials, bulbs and annuals, which look good if arranged in uneven groups. Layer planting is designed to achieve balance and continuity of texture, color and form in the same area.

When designing a planting scheme, leave enough space between plants to develop to their full size. There may be situations when close planting may be used to provide a particular design feature. Plant spacing can depend upon climatic conditions, the soil and the maturity period for the species. Young plants are cheaper, but it may take several years before the planting begins to look mature. The decision to plant a cheaper young specimen or a more mature plant will depend on the budget available. As a general rule, fast-maturing plants and close planting creates a good short-term impact, but more maintenance will be needed in the longer term. A balance between fast- and slow-growing plants will give the most satisfactory results. A number of plants have a striking architectural or sculptural impact. These plants are often used singly as a focal point. They are also effective as part of the design framework. Exotic plants have strong architectural shapes. Many are evergreen and bring a distinctive look to the garden.

Plant selection should also include plants of different bloom cycles. Plants that bloom at different times keep a splash of color in the garden all year. Use plants that are evergreen and semi-evergreen in equally spaced settings for added winter color and unity. Give consideration to plant height. When creating striking color displays keep small plants in front and larger plants in the back but plant height can also be used in creating natural focal points. Native plant selection is also essential. These plants are already adapted to the area. This could amount to a substantial savings not only in plant purchases but in natural resources as well.

L. Shrub beds

Shrub beds form an integral part in the development, renewal and revitalisation of public open areas. Properly designed shrub beds can serve numerous functions providing amenity and quality to the space. Shrub beds should provide spatial definition, visual interest, treatment of slopes, cohesion in the space and a setting for buildings. Other essential points to consider are:

1. Irrigate shrub beds beneath eaves or other overhangs and fencing for the first few years after planting in high use areas to restrict traffic.
2. Use shrub beds on steep slopes unsuitable for grass cover and to reduce erosion caused by storm water.
3. Design beds with adequate surface fall to drain excess water and avoid placing beds in low-lying areas where water cannot easily be removed.
4. Provide shrub planting to attract wildlife and avoid creation of areas for activities such as hiding and loitering.
5. Design shrub beds to allow future vehicular access for mowing, litter removal, tree surgery, pest control and other maintenance and avoid using spiky shrubs near pedestrian areas, playgrounds and high litter areas.
6. Providing windbreaks where winds are likely to make the space unpleasant and avoid obstruction of access to manholes, valves etc.

Shrub beds can be a high maintenance alternative to other landscape options such as dry-land grass. It is necessary to minimise maintenance of the shrub beds. Do not plant shrubs along pedestrian laneways except for specific purposes. The established size of the shrubs should not obstruct sight lines along paths and roadways. Always allow sufficient space for vehicular access to enable future maintenance. Consider the location of existing services such as gas, electricity and telephone lines when designing shrub beds. Shrub plantings between pathways and buildings should not obstruct building maintenance.

M. Safety Considerations

Designing safe environments depends on matching the proper plant to the proper place. Plant characteristics to be considered are whether parts of the plant are poisonous, how much litter the plant produces, the weakness of limbs, whether drooping branches obstruct pathways, whether roots will break pavement, the existence of thorns and whether the plant attracts insects or pests.

Plants with brightly colored poisonous berries or leaves should not be used where children may be tempted to eat them. Some plants can cause an allergic reaction when touched. These should be located out of reach. Plants producing messy fruit or nuts, cones, seed pods or excessive leaf litter are hazardous to pedestrians. They block passage of many wheeled vehicles like strollers and wheelchairs. Large branches are likely to break from wind and ice causing damage and obstruction. Hanging branches into walkways or streets can injure pedestrians and cyclists and may cause damage to larger vehicles. Thorne leaves, twigs and branches that litter the ground can be dangerous for people wearing light shoes or going barefoot. Some people have severe reactions to insect bites and stings. Plants attracting stinging insects or pests should be placed away from sitting areas and walks.

N. Landscape design symbols

Landscape plans use symbols to indicate plants, buildings and other items for information. Symbols are drawn to scale to present an accurate description of the landscape. Symbols used to represent landscape items should be as simple as possible. They should be suggestive of the actual appearance of the landscape features. Color symbols enhance clarity in the landscape plan. Some commonly used symbols are shown below:

1	Deciduous shrub	
2	Deciduous tree	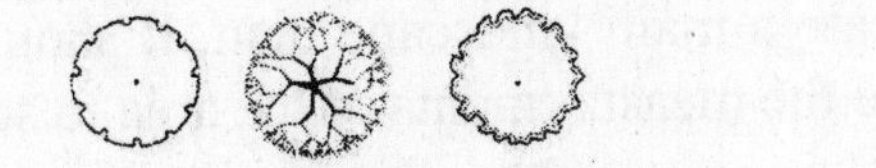
3	Evergreen shrub	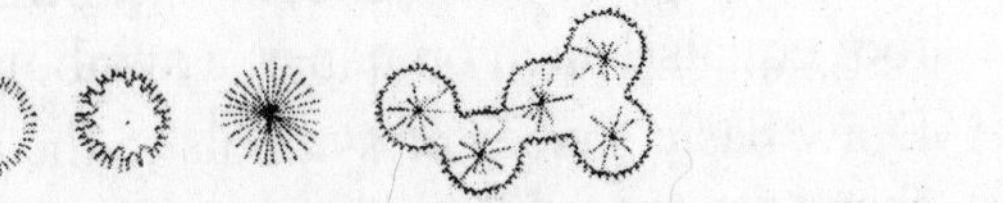
4	Evergreen tree	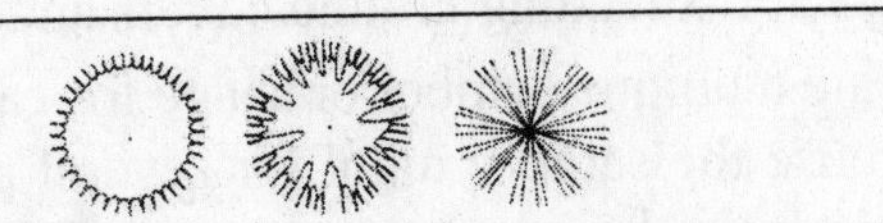
5	Ground covers	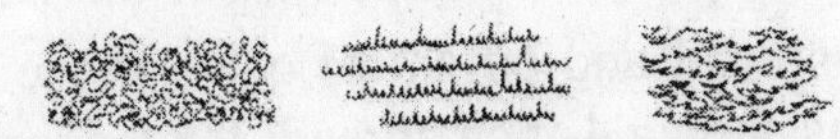
6	Hedge	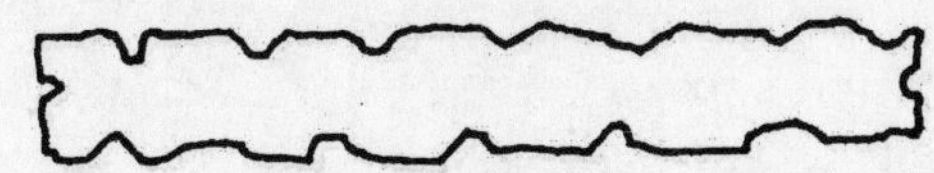
7	Land contours	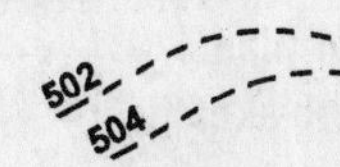
8	Orientation	
9	Ornamental trees	
10	Property line	
11	Turf	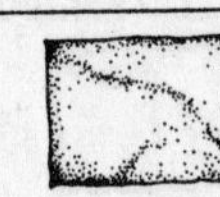
12	Utility lines (s = sewer; w = water supply)	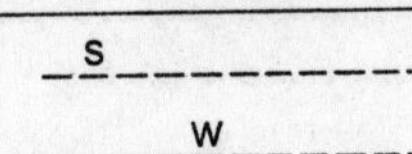

A typical method of drawing landscape plan with symbols is given below:

1. Normally, a landscape plan should cover 3 to 5 years. Changes can be made slowly over time to save costs, or performed all at once.
2. Create a main landscape plan. It should incorporate landmarks of the area and show the boundaries of the area. The plan should note the measurements of the area to scale. Use graph paper to make the scale easy to apply.
3. Draw a scale to the symbols. The scale will depend on the size of the paper and the amount of detail to be shown. For example, if 1 foot equals 1 inch on paper, a symbol for a 6-inch plant would be sized at 1/2-inch for use in the drawing.
4. Draw basic shapes or symbols to the plants in the plan. For example, use circles of varying size to represent trees and shrubs, a 'Y' shape for spreading ground covers and a star or asterisk shape for ornamental grasses.
5. Create a unique symbol or shape for each variety or cultivar of plant in the plan. Use color or a design to differentiate among plants to reuse the same symbol for several plants. Using the leaf shape, branch shape or flower color within the symbol can serve as a reminder and give a better picture of the way the plants may work together visually.
6. Note the spread and height of each of the plants. Base the symbol size on the spread of the mature plant. For smaller plants and flowers, assume a 4-inch spread; for medium sized plants assume a 6-inch spread. Mature shrubs may have a spread of several feet.

EXERCISE

1. What are the Fundamentals of planting design?
2. What is the design role of plants?
3. Explain the following with sketches:
   (*a*) Plant Forms
   (*b*) Plant Texture
   (*c*) Plant Color
   (*d*) Plant Character
4. Highlight few Specimen Trees and Shrubs used in planting design?
5. What are the basics of Tree Planting?
6. Which are the trees commonly seen in India?
7. What care should be taken for plant selection for best landscape design?
8. What are the main safety considerations in planting design?
9. Draw some of the commonly used landscape symbols and the method of drawing landscape plan.

6

Garden Design

While designing a garden, the intention should be to provide a place that satisfies the requirements of those who use it. It is similar to interior designing of a house. Unlike a house, a garden is ever changing. Certain plants may be stunning in one season but not that good in the next season. Three main factors to be considered are:

1. The practical conditions of the site,
2. Its proposed functions,
3. Personal taste

1. Planning

Planning is essential to ensure a consistent design, though much of the pleasure in gardening comes from unpredicted effects. Deciding the basic outline of the garden on paper before making any actual changes will help to avoid costly mistakes. The position of long-term features such as trees, patios and walls should be worked out in advance. Minor alterations can be made later. The garden should be planned as a whole rather than bit by bit. Thus the separate elements are not merely appealing in their own right but effective when viewed as a whole. It is also the time to decide on routine maintenance once the garden is established. It is possible to plan a garden, so that relatively less maintenance is required.

In an existing garden, always spend some time to know the space before re-designing it. Note down the requirements and put together some ideas about the kind of garden wanted. A little patience at the start of the project will save a great deal of confusion and expenditure later. Some plants are not visible at certain times of the year. Most bulbs, appearing in the spring, are gone by the summer. Hardy perennials die down during the winter. It is always sensible to wait before digging the plot. Those sleeping plants could add to the eventual garden design.

When designing a garden, consider it in the context of its immediate surroundings rather than as a stand-alone element. For example, it may be in an elevated position but needs shelter from strong winds. The orientation of the garden - which way it faces in relation to the sun is fundamental to the design. The direction of the sun decides the choice of plants and the best places to sit in the garden. Always remember that the sun travels lower in the sky during the winter. A tree or wall will cast relatively longer shadows in winter than in the summer.

Mark the extent of the shadow patterns at different times of year. It will provide valuable information for planting and designing. Record the details of the views beyond the garden on all sides. A good view can dramatically affect the finished design. Note down the places most affected by the prevailing wind as it may have effect on both plants and people.

2. Modifying an Existing Garden

In the majority of cases, planning involves modifying an existing garden rather than creating a completely new one. There are many reasons to redesign a garden, for example:

1. Change the existing garden design to suit personal taste.
2. The layout of a garden may need to be adapted for a different use like privacy, space for growing vegetables or space for play areas.
3. Reducing the maintenance cost of an existing garden.
4. A neglected garden may need restoration to re-establish.

In an overgrown garden with full of weeds, shrubs and trees do not start work directly and dig up the entire plot. It is better to proceed with care as the garden may be hiding some useful plants to keep. The inclusion of one or two mature specimens in a newly designed garden can provide a framework to design the planting scheme. It is sensible to incorporate the best of the existing features of the garden than forcing a predetermined image on the site. If it is possible, try to live with the garden for a calendar year making notes on any features that may be worth keeping. Take pictures of the garden to catch all four seasons during the first year. These pictures may be taken from ground and first floor windows. They help to identify the good and bad points of the garden.

During this initial period, routine maintenance work like removing perennial weeds, pruning damaged and dead wood from shrubs and trees, cutting grass and clipping hedges should be carried out to keep the garden in good condition. Overgrown hedges can be restored over a period of time by trimming and pruning. Safe old trees can be given a new lease of life as support for climbing plants, climbing frames, space for hillocks and swings to hang. They may provide shade and good screening from wind and ugly views. Shrubs can be moved. Many can withstand a hard pruning. A thumb rule is to look at the base of the plant, if it has just one stem; it is not likely to grow out new roots. Herbaceous plants can be revived by dividing the original old bunch. One of the major challenges in renovating an old garden is dealing with established weeds. The weeds in the soil may be dealt either organically using fabric mulch over a period of time or by using a chemical weed-killer.

3. Designing a New Garden

Making a garden on a brand new site is an exciting challenge. Starting with a blank canvas gives more freedom to include the design elements of choice and removes the constraints of an existing garden. It is important to remember that the garden should be designed in relation to its setting. Factors such as climate and soil type should be taken into account. It is useful to sketch a rough outline of the garden site. Note down the main elements to be included. Mark fixed features like the position of the house and the boundaries. Allocate approximate areas for borders, beds, patio, lawn, pool or any other features needed. Make room for functional fixtures like a tool shed or compost heap. These items should be located away from the house.

In landscaping gardens, there should be number of specimen trees in all large plantings to show their individual good qualities. The selection of suitable trees is most important. Shrubs are indispensable in all types of gardening. A study of the species and varieties is essential. Hardy perennials may be used in almost any situation where plants are wanted. They may grow under the trees, among the shrubs, in rockeries, along the borders of ponds, on sloping banks, in shade or sun. The annuals have great variety and adaptability to all needs and circumstances making them always indispensable. Round plants have the same capabilities as the herbaceous perennials. Many of them will live without protection and thrive year after year. Some require winter protection, but last without replanting for many years. The climbers are useful for buildings, fences and to cover unsightly objects. They are also useful for shading and decoration of porches.

4. Deciding on the Garden Style

There are many types of garden styles, but personal taste is the main deciding factor. One need not limit to just one style of garden. It is possible to combine elements of two or three different types or create something entirely new.

Cottage garden has an informal layout and contains many interesting and unusual plants. It may also include some wild or conservation areas and a water feature. It needs good maintenance and horticultural expertise. Whatever may be the style, few basic design principles should be observed. Harmony and balance are essential. Try to include features that complement each other. The overall setting should produce a cohesive design. Always choose a garden style that does not require repeated mowing, clipping, weeding, staking and tidying to remain beautiful.

Fig. 6.1. Typical Pot garden

Fig. 6.2. Typical Walled garden

Fig. 6.3. Typical Herb garden

5. Creating Functional Areas

Make sure that each space performs its designed function. Thinking about how the garden will be enjoyed and used is all part of good garden design. While building a pond, there should be space to sit, relax and watch the fish. While locating a compost heap, there should be easy access. Planting areas need to be planned for easy maintenance. Consider the boundaries as an important part of the overall design. The following space guidelines help to create a garden, which looks beautiful and works efficiently.

1. The height of barbecues and work tops should be 75 to 85 cm (30-33 in). Position them carefully in relation to sun, wind and neighbors property.
2. Boundary walls can cast rain shadows on beds below them. Hedges planted at the backs of borders need to have 30 cm (1 ft) access behind the planting for maintenance.

3. Lawns need to be in sun or light shade. The seed mixture or turf should be chosen accordingly. It is good to construct a mowing edge to the lawn with brick or other frost-proof material.
4. Pergolas and arches should be high enough for adequate head clearance. A head room of 2.1 m (7 ft) is essential.
5. The minimum size for a patio or terrace is 3.6 × 3.6 m (12 × 12 ft). It gives enough space for a moderate table and four chairs.
6. All surfaces should be at least 2 courses of brick below the building damp proof course (15 cm or 6 in).
7. Paving should fall gently from the building (not less than 1:100) to avoid water running towards the foundations of the building.
8. Paths should be no less than 60 cm (2 ft) wide. For access to wheeled toys and barrows 1 m (3 ft) is required.
9. The average garden pond need not to be more than 60 cm (2 ft) deep, with marginal shelves 22 cm (9 in) below the surface. Shelves should be approximately 30 cm (1 ft) wide.
10. Pools should be placed in full sun for water plants, but away from deciduous trees, which may drop leaves into the water.
11. Seating should be approximately 45 cm (18 in) high.
12. Steps should have normally a riser height of 15 cm (6 in) and a tread of 45 cm (18 in). The maximum gradient of a ramp should be not more than 1:10.

6. Hiding ugly views

Many gardens have ugly views inside and outside. It is possible to hide both. The most simple and effective way is to use plants to hide or screen. Boundaries can be a real problem. Consider planting tall evergreen plants in front of high overshadowing walls to soften them or use the wall as a screen to paint interesting scenes. Manholes are usually located near the building. To mask, use inset covers that can put temporary paving over it. At times manholes are positioned right in the middle of the lawn. Simply stand a pot or other ornament on it to hide it. In the border areas they can be covered with low spreading plants. Garden sheds can be screened with shrubs or a hedge Dustbins can be hidden with brick, stone or timber enclosures. Compost heaps should be located in a corner of the garden. It is better to create an area for both dustbin and compost bin.

7. Assessing the Site

An initial assessment forms the basis of a scale drawing. Survey should include factors such as climate and soil type in addition to detailed measurements of the site. This information is very useful to locate shelter, drainage and plants. Always take professional help to prepare a scale plan. After taking the measurements of the site, the location of drains, manholes, ventilation pipes and septic tank covers should be noted. Fix their position and make a note of their exact size and angle. Ensure that all walls, patios, paths, pools, greenhouse and pergolas have been included in the plan. Indicate the materials of these structures and their condition. Note the condition of the lawn, perennial plants, trees, shrubs and hedges and work out pruning or renovation needed. Make an estimate of the current and ultimate sizes of the trees and shrubs. This information will help to decide which plants to remove or relocate, and other hard elements to keep or modify. Note down significant level changes at the survey stage as the new design may have to include certain features to include the gradient. A gentle downwards slope away from the building facilitates drainage for a patio or lawn. However, a steep sloping garden may need retaining walls or terraces.

When planning a garden use natural site features as part of the design wherever possible. Banks, slopes and changes in level may provide chance to create retaining walls, terraces, a watercourse, stepped beds, a rock garden or good views out of the garden. Poorly drained and damp areas are difficult and expensive to drain. Make a building for many bog and moisture-loving plants. If large areas of subsoil or rubble are left after construction, they may be used to form the base of a gravel garden than replacing them with good soil. Gravel gardens require minimal maintenance once they are established.

8. Climate Considerations

When planning a garden, it will be useful to find out local annual rainfall, sunshine hours, temperatures and any other special climatic influences. Climatic variations will depend on latitude, altitude and a number of other local factors. The geographical setting may also make a difference. Hilltop sites over 150-200 m (480-640 ft) above sea-level may be colder than nearby low-lying places. Coastal gardens are susceptible to salt-laden winds. Town gardens are usually warmer than those in rural areas.

The microclimate should be considered in planning a garden. Note which way the garden faces and which parts receive most shade and sun at different times of day and different seasons of a year. Try to take advantage of the different microclimates within the garden growing plants that enjoy the available conditions than trying to cultivating unsuitable species. It is always better to work with nature than fight against it. It means growing plants that enjoy the given conditions than struggling to nurture inappropriate species. The following guidelines are useful with regard to the microclimate conditions.

1. Take the sun position into account while planning the garden. The exact location of the sun in the garden in different seasons and times of the day is very important. Plan patios and places to sit and relax in both summer and winter based on sun movement within the garden.
2. Garden orientation and elevation will affect planting. Gardens on a hill will affect the levels of temperature, light and wind. Gardens with north facing slopes have less sunshine. South facing slopes receive more sun light and heat, and plant growth will be earlier.
3. Always choose plants from climates and habitats similar to existing garden for lower maintenance and a higher success rates.
4. Use existing walls and fences to best advantage when choosing plants. North facing walls will provide a constantly cool and shaded spot. South facing walls will be sunny, hot and dry. East facing walls are moist and cool. West facing walls are warm.
5. Try to filter, baffle and drain than contain wind. Choose hedges such as picket or ranch types rather than solid panels. Choose sheltered sites to sit. Wind causes physical damage to plants, so install a temporary shelter around new trees and shrubs to help them get established.
6. Position kitchen gardens to receive sun to warm up the soil early in the season and avoid placing near frost pockets.
7. Planting around hot walls and patios need care because heat reflected by the paved surface can burn some plant foliage Use deciduous plants to shade patios and the house from hot summer sun. Their bare branches in winter will allow winter sun to warm up the garden.

9. Soil

It is essential to find the type, texture and acidity level (pH) of the soil. Soils may be light, sandy, heavy clay, chalky or acidic. The soil type affects the type of plants to be grown. It also affects drainage, digging and planting. Check the level of water found naturally in the ground at different times of the year by digging trial holes in different parts of the garden. Most plant roots grow in the top 45 cm (18 in) of soil.

10. Cost

Hard landscape features like paving and walling can take up to 75% of the total costs. It is worth doing some market research to check the price of materials. Paving slabs vary enormously in cost. As a general rule, natural paving is more expensive than man-made. The larger the size of each paving element, the cheaper it is to lay. In trying to reduce the cost of the design, always remember that plants, seeds and turf are all relatively inexpensive and do not require labor.

11. Xeriscape Gardening

Xeriscaping means water efficient landscaping. The term xeriscape is derived from the Greek word xeros, which means dry. It is not a style of garden design. It is a method of gardening that involves choosing plants appropriate to their site and creating a landscape, maintained with little additional watering. By grouping plants by their water needs, using mulch and drought tolerant plants, water can be saved. It also leads to healthier gardens needing less use of fertilizers and pesticides.

The basic guidelines for Xeriscaping are:

1. Plan garden based on topography, sun exposure and soil. Create planting zones and group plants by their needs. Group the tough, drought tolerant plants in areas exposed to full day sun. Give less tolerant plants some partial shade. Keep the delicate plants near water source. Select most of the native plants which thrive with low water conditions. Try to integrate very few plants needing comparatively more water.

Fig. 6.4. Typical Xeriscape Garden

Fig. 6.5. Typical Orgainic garden

2. Take proper care of the soil by incorporating generous amounts of organic matter. This will improve water holding and penetration in any type of soil. Water holding soil will promote good root development and reduces the need for additional water.

3. Mulching is a naturally occurring process. It controls soil temperature, holds moisture, slows erosion and suppresses weeds. It also gradually decomposes and feeds the soil. At the initial planting stage apply about 4 inches of mulch and check each season for refilling.
4. The placement of lawn should be part of initial design plan. Think about how much water and fertilizer is taken to keep the lawn green throughout the summer. Choose an appropriate grass seed for the lawn exposure. Different seeds do well in different regions. There are other options less labor and water intensive than grass as a ground cover.
5. All plants do not need the same amount of water. Water needs may change with the seasons. Drip irrigation systems are often recommended for efficient watering. All plants need watering for the first one or two years. Watering should become much less frequent after they have acclimatized and developed a good root system.
6. Watering, weeding, pruning, deadheading and sensible pest management is necessary for good garden. Many plants will grow in drought conditions, if they have been selected wisely. No plant will survive forever without some water. Different plants will thrive in different regions and conditions.

EXERCISE

1. How do you plan a garden?
2. How do you modify an existing garden?
3. How do you design a new garden?
4. How do you decide on the Garden Style to be adopted?
5. How do you create 'Functional Areas' in a garden?
6. Explain the importance of the following in garden design
   (*a*) Views
   (*b*) Site
   (*c*) Climate
   (*d*) Soil
   (*e*) Cost
7. What is Xeriscape Gardening?

7
Garden Styles

There is no clear definition for any one style and every style is open to interpretation by gardeners everywhere. Even the same style can be identified differently between continents. A cottage garden style in the United Kingdom (UK) can be very different from the cottage garden in Russia. Similarly in any country there may be different styles according to the natural environment in which they are built. For example in the UK there is a 'seaside garden' and a 'woodland garden', while in the USA, they have East Coast, West Coast, Southern and Prairie styles and in Africa they have the tropical garden style or their individualistic desert style which is derived from the beaten red earth, native pots and tough desert plants.

Whatever may be the garden style it is closely linked to what is available in any particular locality. Tall buildings around a garden give an enclosed impression and different gardeners may tackle the same situation differently. Some may try to create a more 'open' outlook, while others create an enclosed garden style. Colours appearing fantastic under strong sunlight do not have the same effect under a cloudy sky.

The following are some normal garden styles:

1. Cottage Garden
2. Arid Garden
3. Fern Garden
4. Herb & kitchen Garden
5. Rock Garden
6. Roof Garden
7. Japanese Garden
   - Tsukiyama gardens (Hill Gardens)
   - Karesansui gardens (dry gardens)
   - Chaniwa gardens (tea gardens)

1. Cottage Garden

The cottage garden design is based on an informal abundance of flowers. Traditionally, such profusion of planting completely surrounded a small cottage in the country. The term reminds different images depending upon each ones national viewpoint. The cottage garden style is difficult to define because it can be different things to different people. For some the romantic cottage garden style includes a small cottage in the country, mixing up roses over an arch and a winding path into the woods beyond. For others there must be a profusion of informal, mixed planting, wild flowers and a vegetable patch at the bottom.

Fig. 7.1. Typical Cottage garden

A cottage garden design style needs more control and work than other. There should be a relaxed, informal planting with the emphasis on dense planting and permanent borders. It requires a strong theme and a strong framework. The colours of plants should reflect and harmonise with local colours. Sometimes the cottage garden style may look haphazard and incoherent because many gardeners plant anything as long as the planting is dense and full of variety.

The 'natural look' can easily eliminate the essential tasks of weeding and pruning which are necessary in a cottage garden. The 'natural look' can work well for a few years before nature reclaims her own, and as the natural look garden loses its direction it becomes lost in a haphazard mix of general untidiness and complacency. The original cottage gardens were created by working-class country people who spend many hours maintaining their plot in order to feed themselves and provide personal pleasure. They cared for their plants over many hours and this style requires a keen and enthusiastic gardener to maintain it.

The garden design style at Winsford Walled Garden in London, UK draws heavily from the cottage garden style. Its magnificent Victorian garden walls are decorated with sub-tropical climbers. There is a hidden world of protective shrubs and unusual perennials among sublime hard landscaping like the circular brick patio with the brick pathway. There are great columns up to 6 inches thick rising from the ground. Once in a while one of the twelve coniferous steeples will burst the planting heading skywards. A 5ft wide winding path runs through it like a country stream opening new vistas at every turn. Some borders are up to 30ft deep. All of them are mixed and packed with unusual herbaceous perennials and shrubs. The general theme of individual spaces running through the gardens is both harmonious and practical because there are no distinct hedges creating definitive garden rooms. These spaces are like the pages of a book, moving from one garden section to another. Visitors can view the individual spaces and can easily imagine the same in their own plot.

Some guidelines for creating an interesting 'Cottage garden' are given below:

1. Have a patio made out of a mixture of materials laid in a random pattern. Use recycled or salvaged materials to achieve an instant worn look.
2. Make sure lawn fits into the cottage garden picture. Leave grass a little longer and allow flowers to remain. Go for a wild flower meadow look with minimal mowing control.
3. Try to make arches supporting climbing plants look as rustic as possible. Use rustic treated posts for real authenticity.

4. Recycled beams and timbers are good for cottage garden. Make simple arches, panels for dividing areas, border edges and plant supports out of woven willow or dogwoods.
5. Choose garden seats and other furniture in rustic looking timber.
6. Make water features such as pools useful to dip watering cans.
7. Make compost bins look like bee hives. Cordon off utility areas using hurdles.
8. Try using half barrels, terracotta pots or old crockery for planted containers. Old baskets to cover plastic pots.
9. Grow fruit and vegetable crops amongst ornamental plants.
10. Pack plants close together to keep down weeds.
11. Include low growing plants at the front of borders to grow over the edge of paving and hide edges.
12. Grow climbing and scrambling plants through hedges, shrubs and trees.
13. Plant topiary shapes using faster growing plants for quick results.

Fig. 7.2. Typical Arid garden

Fig. 7.3. Typical Fern garden

2. Arid Garden

The arid garden style could well become increasingly practical as the threat of global warming continues to affect us all. The dry garden does not have to be desert looking. It can be vibrant and colourful. The dry arid garden is a style of gardening in areas which are short of rainfall.

There are many styles to choose, which have evolved over the years. The dry garden style designer can use the garden styles of more southerly gardens as a starting point and move them north adapting them to fit the new location. Inspiration for dry or arid garden style can be drawn from the garden styles of Mexico, Spain, North Africa, the Mediterranean and Arabia.

The main focus of these garden styles is the courtyard, a space at the back, front or even side of a home can be used for these type of gardens. These types of gardens create a sanctuary away from the blazing heat of the sun and the bustling traffic beyond. Vibrant colours are often used in these gardens to offset the bright sun light.

3. Fern Garden

No plant gives a greater feeling of cooling and calmness than the fern. Ferns have a tranquil aura. They provide great diversity and form. They can comfortably grow and excel in locations where normal sun needing plants do not grow. During the 19th century, Victorian fern gardens were often tucked away beneath the shade of mature trees. By the 1870's the increase of fern nurseries and the demand for ferns was having a serious impact upon the available national natural stock. There are approximately 12,000 species of fern around the world today. They grow naturally in forest, the banks of waterways, upon walls and mountainside. In fact they grow naturally anywhere.

Ferns can grow anywhere provided they have unrestricted access to moisture during their growing season. If an individual fern is short of the essential moisture, it can quickly dehydrate. To create any fern garden

(*a*) provide the moisture in the first place,

(*b*) provide sufficient shade to reduce the evaporation of that moisture to a minimum.

Ferns prefer humus rich compost to retain the moisture. At the same time they prefer free-draining compost that enables air to reach the roots and prevent rotting. Identify the existing conditions of the proposed fern garden and then the ferns suitable to those conditions. Find out whether the proposed fernery contains acid, neutral or alkaline soil because it affects the growth of ferns. Majority of ferns prefer slightly acidic soil. An ideal soil composition consists of 20% clay, 30% grit and 50% sand. This provides the best balance of anchorage, moisture retention and free draining soil. Avoid planting ferns in the winter. Ferns prefer rainwater wherever possible. Fern care is easy and mainly involves removing damaged leaves and any debris littering the crown. Ferns do not require any supplemental feeding.

4. Herb & kitchen Garden

Herbs are undemanding plants. The herb garden design style is an easy one. All herbs need a bit of sunshine. It is necessary to bed their roots in some well-drained soil, which need not be nutritious. Herb gardens were the first ever gardens. Herb gardens are simple areas within easy reach of the kitchen for the benefit of the household. It was the same during the time of the ancient Greeks and Romans and it remains the same today.

Fig. 7.4. Typical Herb & Kitchen garden

The traditional herb garden is an arrangement of small, regular beds in a geometric shape. Square, diamond and triangular shapes are frequently used. The French Parterre is a level garden, usually rectangular and divided easily into ornamental beds. Modern formal herb garden is normally based on a single focal point. It may be a statue, bird bath or a sundial. Herbs need protection from the winds because of their warm climate origins. Neat box hedging has become an essential part of every herb garden design. Each bed can be filled with all types of herbs or small quantities of vegetables. Herbs can be divided into different groups such as those for flavoring, garnishing, and sweet smelling or medicinal. Anyone can grow herbs in a plot size of six square feet and provides fresh produce throughout the summer.

Garlic (Allium sativum) is one of the most widely grown herbs in the garden. The apparent odour and taste of fresh basil (*Ocimum basilicum*) makes any good salad a great salad. Although very tender, basil can be started under cover and transferred outside for the summer. The delicious leaves and young stalks of lovage (*Levisticum officinale*) are slightly nutty to taste and make a good herb for the pot. Even the roots can be stripped to add flavour to casseroles. Oregano or pot marjoram (*Origanum vulgare*) is another Mediterranean region native. It's fresh leaves are used as ingredients to French and especially Italian cooking. Thyme (*Thymus vulgaris*) is another fragrant herb which is synonymous with Pizza. Thyme is low growing and looks like a rich colourful carpet when in flower. Fresh mint (*Mentha spicata*) makes a refreshing drink at any time. It will take over if planted in open ground. Plant any mint (*i.e.* peppermint, spearmint) in a pot in order to restrict its root growth. Sage (*Salvia officinalis*) is another mediterranean aromatic herb, which is very useful in the kitchen. It is often used in association with onion for flavouring meats, especially pork and poultry.

5. Rock Garden

A rock garden features extensive use of rocks or stones along with native plants. Rock garden plants tend to be small because many of the species are naturally small to avoid covering up the rocks. They can be grown in troughs and containers or in the ground. The plants prefer well-drained soil and less water.

The usual form of a rock garden is a pile of rocks, large and small, aesthetically arranged with small gaps in between, where the plants are rooted. Some rock gardens may also incorporate bonsai. Many rock gardens are designed and built to look like natural outcrops of bedrock. Stones are aligned to suggest a bedding plane and plants are often used to conceal the joints between the stones. This type of rockery was popular in Victorian times.

Fig. 7.5. Typical Rock garden

Fig. 7.6. Typical Roof garden

6. Roof Garden

Gardening areas are rarely found in cities, which is one of the main reasons that rooftop and balcony gardens have become so popular. Many of the same design considerations apply to these gardens even though roof gardens are often more exposed to the sun and wind than patios. Low-maintenance design and planting is often the highest design priority. The weight of containers is also important, if there are weight restrictions. Plastic or fibre-glass containers are preferable than terracotta or stone. Lightweight materials should be used in place of heavy paving slabs for additional flooring area. Provide shelter for plants and people with sturdy trellis screens to withstand strong winds. Any windbreaks must be securely fixed for safety reasons.

Balconies are often more sheltered than roof gardens. They are frequently shaded from above. The available space may be best used by growing climbers and by fixing sturdy brackets and shelves to the house wall to support troughs and pots of trailing plants. Temperatures will be approximately 5°C higher than the air temperature at ground level. Roof garden plants need to be tolerant of high levels of sun, wind and drought.

A roof garden needs careful thought. Take specialist advice before starting work. One advantage of roof gardens is that they always have wide views. This also means that the garden will be windier than at ground level, and will face greater extremes of temperature. Check planning or conservation area controls do not apply to the proposed new roof garden. The structural strength of the roof must be surveyed. It must be capable of supporting the additional weight of the garden. While planning the roof garden access will be restricted. Everything in the rooftop garden must be brought up through a living area into the garden. Safety is an important consideration. Every feature must be securely and safely fitted. Containers should not be placed where there is danger of them being blown away.

Always consider reducing the weight when choosing materials. Timber and plastic are useful for screens and other structures. Canvas awnings provide good instant shaded spaces. Decking is a good choice for seating areas. Fibreglass artificial rocks look realistic and light for making natural features. Galvanised metal may be used for containers and raised beds. Beds and containers should be lined and given adequate base drainage before filling with a lightweight-planting medium.

7. Japanese Garden

The Japanese garden style is a highly controlled style of garden design, which strives to be a symbolic representation of nature itself. People appreciate the calming influence when gazing upon a Japanese garden style scene. The inherent simplicity of the Japanese garden style is not its only advantage, it is a garden style that can fit in to any suburban space and does not require a great amount of regular garden maintenance - like weeding.

It is a garden style, which if it is to be truly authentic needs to build according to strict rules. The great Japanese gardens have evolved over a great length of time with the traditional Japanese religion of Shinto having a strong influence. These factors are rarely appreciated by western gardeners who wish to build a Japanese style garden.

History and politics influenced the japanese garden. The ancient Asuka period (552-644A.D.) had gardens with Chinese symbolism. Prior to this, the people believed that the landscape was filled with spirits or 'kami' mountains, commonly represented in the garden, were the dwelling place of the kami, (sacred mountains are conical in shape; hence Mt. Fuji is most sacred). Stones were also the home of the kami. During Nara period (645-782 A.D.), Buddhism arrived in japan. This brought about the depiction of human elements in the garden. The Heian period (784-1183 A.D.) gardens were revered as paradise and flowers were introduced into the garden.The kimono also started having flower prints. During this period, Saku teiki wrote a book on gardening describing how to use stone, water, trees, etc. He gives 138 ways to place stones in the garden. This Gardening Manual is supposed to be the oldest one in world history of landscape. During the Kamakura period (1183 to 1333 A.D.), Zen buddhism emphasized contemplation and meditation. The golden pavilion at Kinkakuji and the Moss Garden at saihoji, where more than 50 species of moss were grown, are two examples of garden from this period.

During the Muromachi period (1394-1572 A.D.) the famous Ryoan-ji temple Garden was built and the emergence of abstraction is seen. The religion of Japan had emphasized on the elements of the universe. The primitive Japanese worshipped the sun, the moon, the mountains, the stones, etc.

In Japan, the garden is always nature oriented, e.g. bonsai is a garden in miniature; bonseki is a landscape in miniature; ikebana, etc. During Momoyama period (1573-1602 A.D.), evergreens and their shaping were introduced into the garden and Azaleas was a common plant. Stone lanterns were another element from this period. During Edo period (1605-1867 A.D.) the Katsura Imperial Villa was built and is a good example of a water garden.

The raked gravel in Japanese style gardens symbolises the movement of water amidst rock islands. The movement of the wavy gravel counters the dramatic still and calm of the carefully placed rock Timber beams creating a footpath on stilts can symbolise a great journey over many difficulties. Bamboo is often used in Japanese style garden design. Large canes are both dramatic and last many years and can be used as low fences beside footpaths and gravel features. Water is a popular feature of so many Japanese garden style designs, barely moving, it's often used for reflective effect-both visually and mentally. There are many Japanese lantern designs each with a particular significance. Pedestal Lanterns or *Rankei*, should be used adjacent to water so the lantern itself can extend over water for its reflective beauty. Pagoda lanterns or *Kasuga*, are majestic and should dominate the area.

There are three basic Japanese garden styles: Tsukiyama gardens (Hill Gardens), Karesansui Gardens (dry gardens) and Chaniwa Gardens (tea gardens).

Fig. 7.7. Typical Tsukiyama garden

1. **Tsukiyama gardens** (Hill Gardens): Ponds, streams, hills, stones, trees, flowers, bridges and paths are used to create a miniature reproduction of natural scenery which is often a famous landscape in China or Japan. The name Tsukiyama refers to the creation of artificial hills. Tsukiyama gardens vary in size and in the way they are viewed. Smaller gardens are usually enjoyed from a single viewpoint, such as the veranda of a temple, while many larger gardens are best experienced by following a circular scrolling path.
2. **Karesansui Gardens** (dry gardens): Karesansui gardens reproduce natural landscapes in a more abstract way by using stones, gravel, sand and sometimes a few patches of moss for representing mountains, islands, boats, seas and rivers. Karesansui gardens are strongly influenced by Zen Buddhism and used for meditation.
3. **Chaniwa Gardens** (tea gardens): Chaniwa gardens are built for the tea ceremony. They contain a tea house where the actual ceremony is held and are designed in aesthetic simplicity according to the concepts of sado (tea ceremony). Chaniwa gardens typically feature stepping stones that lead towards the tea house, stone lanterns and a stone basin (tsukubai), where guests purify themselves before participating in the ceremony.

Fig. 7.8. Typical Karesansui Garden

Fig. 7.9. Typical Chaniwa Garden (tea garden)

EXERCISE

1. Describe the following garden styles
   (*a*) Cottage Garden
   (*b*) Arid Garden
   (*c*) Fern Garden
   (*d*) Herb & kitchen Garden
   (*e*) Rock Garden
   (*f*) Roof Garden
   (*g*) Japanese Garden

8

Plant Management

Plant management may include many things, but primarily Landscape designer has to deal with problems caused by plant pests and weeds, diseases and disorders. With careful planting and management majority of these problems may be avoided. Optimum growing conditions will ensure that plants remain healthy resisting diseases and pests. Good plant management involves spotting and preventing plant problems at an early stage when they can be treated more easily.

The number of pests, weeds and diseases can be minimised by following the basics of good plant hygiene practices. Weeding thoroughly, clearing up leaves, removing dead wood and pruning prevents the shelter and nourishment found by pests amongst weeds and debris. Pests and diseases cause most of the problems with plants. Keeping plants healthy and growing strongly can help them resist problems. If plants are affected by pests or diseases, think carefully before going for chemical spray because some pests may not be hazardous. There are other alternatives to chemical treatment like biological and organic practices to preserve the natural ecosystem.

The following methods may be used to prevent pests and diseases to plants:

1. **Prevention of Pests and Diseases:** The old proverb 'prevention is better than cure' applies well to plants and the fight against pests and diseases. Being vigilant and carrying out good hygienic practices can help preventing diseases and pests affecting the plants.
2. **Landscape Hygiene:** Plant hygiene is one of the strongest weapons against the risk of pests and diseases. It means removing general debris and weeds on a regular basis to prevent them from becoming a refuge for pests and weeds. It is also important to remove and burn diseased material to stop it spreading to other plants. Plant pots and other equipment like knifes should be cleaned between use to avoid infections and diseases spreading from plant to plant.
3. **Keeping Plants Healthy:** Strong and healthy plants are less likely to be infected than weak and unhealthy ones. Always purchase plants which appear vigorous and healthy with no signs of dying down, abnormally coloured leaves or poor root development. Consider buying disease-resistant varieties of plants. Always try to grow plants in the right conditions taking into account the soil type, texture and pH, the amount of sunlight and exposure to frost or wind. A plant grown in proper environment will have a much better chance of resisting any problems.
4. **Plant spacing:** Plant spacing is another important consideration in planting. Crowded planting will not only lead to plants competing for nutrients, air, water and light, but the close, humid surroundings encourage fungal disease. If a plant is badly

damaged by disease or pests, it is better to destroy it to avoid infecting other healthy plants.

5. **Natural Predators:** It is worth encouraging helpful natural predators to prevent plant problems because they help in pest control. There are a number of beneficial pest predators such as hoverflies, ladybirds, lacewings, frogs, toads and hedgehogs; which can control flies, beetles, grubs and slugs to a manageable level. Pest predators may be encouraged by providing food plants and shelter. For example, hoverflies can be attracted by planting French marigolds, which they visit for nectar, while slug-eating ground beetles enjoy the shelter that can be provided with mulches and thick planting. Some birds, such as blackbirds, blue tits and thrushes enjoy feeding on insect's pests, and may be encouraged with water, food in the winter, and nesting boxes.

Any controlling measures taken against pests should not harm the beneficial insects and animals. Persistent chemical control can wipe out the natural predators and making the plant more vulnerable to attacks and infestation.

A. Organic Control

There has been a widespread interest in organic gardening because it uses as few manufactured chemicals as possible. The broad philosophy behind organic gardening is to take a holistic view of gardening. This means:

1. Striving to conserve natural resources.
2. Understanding the interdependence of all life forms in the garden.
3. Avoiding pollution and health hazards.
4. Establishing a balanced ecological habitat for plants, animals and humans.

Organic control can be achieved in a number of ways using natural methods to help plants resist and recover from attack by pests and diseases.

1. **Disease-Resistant Plants:** Some varieties of plants are specifically bred to resist certain pests or diseases. Check if there are disease or pest resistant varieties are available before buying plants.
2. **Plant Health:** Keeping plants healthy can prevent a number of infections and infestations. Grow seedlings in pots so that they are protected properly. Make sure that only healthy and vigorous stock is planted out. Maintaining a good spacing between plants will allow them to grow without overcrowding. It also helps to prevent fungal diseases. Check plants regularly for signs of problems. A well-established infection is more difficult to deal with than one that is identified and treated early.
3. **Mulching:** The addition of moisture-retaining protective covering can help to keep powdery mildew from crops and ornamentals.
4. **Companion Planting:** Positioning certain plants together can reduce pest and disease attack. This is especially true of herbs, whose strong scents can repel pests or attract them away from more important planting. They can also attract beneficial insects that will act as natural predators. For example, chives, fennel and oregano all repel aphids, while coriander and mint attract natural insect predators.
5. **Garden Hygiene:** Regularly removing and burning any infested or diseased plants or material will help to reduce the risk of the problem spreading. At the same time destroying or composting garden waste will prevent it from becoming a refuge for pests.
6. **Crop Rotation:** Growing the same plant in one area for a number of years can lead to soil-borne pests and diseases of that plant. This may be relieved by rotating the crops and growing other botanically unrelated plants. Although crop rotation is most often

carried out in the vegetable garden, it may also be used for annuals, bulbs and other plants.

7. **Organic Treatment:** There are some chemical treatments that derive from natural sources, such as derris dust, soft soap, sulphur dust and pyrethrum (from the pyrethrum daisy). Although they are safe to use, they only act on contact with the disease or pest, so regular applications are needed.
8. **Organic Traps:** Traps may be easily put together to catch a wide range of pests.
   (*a*) Trap earwigs in inverted flower pots.
   (*b*) Attract wireworms to cut potatoes or carrot buried 10-15 cm (4-6 in) deep.
   (*c*) Use beer traps to catch slugs.
   (*d*) Attract greenhouse whitefly to a yellow card smeared with grease.

B. Biological Control

Biological control involves keeping down pests by the introduction of natural enemies: predators, parasites and diseases. This technique may be essential in the greenhouse, where pests may have developed immunity to chemicals.

A. **Control in the Greenhouse:** The biological control is very attractive and it is becoming more popular. There are now several different pest predators available to kill whiteflies, red spider mites, mealybugs, leaf miners, scale insects, thrips and vine weevils. Biological controls are particularly useful in the greenhouse. Its controlled, warm environment and excellent light allows predators and parasites to breed faster than pests. It is important to introduce the control before plants are heavily infested otherwise it may take a number of weeks to become effective. The majority of parasites and predators need temperatures of at least 21°C (70°F) for at least part of the day and good sunlight. They should be released onto the affected plants in the cooler part of the day on the day of occurrence. Some predators are strong fliers, so open doors and windows need to be netted to prevent them from escaping.

B. **Control in the Garden:** Many of the biological controls are only suitable for use in the greenhouse or conservatory. There are other biological controls which may be used outdoors. These are natural predators like birds, hedgehogs and frogs which should be encouraged to visit the garden. Harmful insects can be reduced by spiders, frogs, ants, wasps and birds, whilst hedgehogs, shrews, frogs and toads feed on many plant pests. The centipede is also a useful ally, feeding on soil-dwelling pests.

C. Chemical Control

If pests and diseases cannot be prevented or treated by using proper cultivation methods and organic control, then it may be necessary to treat them with chemicals. A careful combination of organic and chemical techniques may provide the best solution to difficult and recurrent problems.

1. **Pesticides and Fungicides:** Pesticides are used to kill insects, mites and other pests. Fungicides are used to control diseases caused by fungi. Both types work either by contact action or systemically. Contact pesticides kill pests when they are hit by the chemical during spraying or when they later crawl over a treated plant. Systemic pesticides are drawn up through the roots or taken in through the leaf pores and then transported by the sap stream throughout the entire plant. This makes pesticides of this type particularly useful for sap-suckers. Although contact fungicides kill germinating fungal spores and prevent further infection, they have little effect on established fungal growths. A systemic fungicide is needed to kill fungi in the plant tissues.

2. **Ingredients and Formulations:** Pesticides and fungicides can be bought in a range of different formulations like concentrated liquids, dusts, powders, smoke and pre-diluted sprays. Always avoid making more concentrates than necessary because they may become ineffective within 24 hours. It is best to buy ready-made sprays for smaller areas. These sprays last as long as undiluted concentrates and do not need to be mixed.
3. **Chemical Safety:** While working with chemicals, it is necessary to minimise any harm to the user or to the environment. Always read the information on the label, carefully follow the instructions and never exceed the recommended dose. Any pesticide which may be potentially harmful to bees and other beneficial insects should only be sprayed in the late evening when they are no longer working the flowers. Carefully follow the instructions for disposal of excess chemicals. They should never be poured down sinks, drains or watercourses.

D. Plant Care

Plants damaged by diseases or pests should be fed with a general fertilizer after an attack to restore them to health. Use a foliar feed for root damage. Root damage makes uptake of nutrients from the soil difficult.

1. **Pests:** A garden pest is any animal or insect causing damage to plants. The damage may be by chewing leaves, sucking sap, removing bark or tunnelling through leaves, fruits or stems. Many pests can also damage plants by spreading viral or fungal diseases. Some other pests like aphids, coat the plant in a sticky substance encouraging the growth of sooty moulds.
2. **Weeds:** Weeds are plants growing where they should not grow. They are often fast-growing, persistent and survive in almost any soil. Their drawback is that they fight with cultivated plants for space, light, water and food. Ornamental cultivated plants can also be classed as weeds, if they are persistent for their site or self-seed freely throughout the garden.
3. **Types of Weeds:** There are two major types of weed: yearly and perennial.
   - Yearly weeds complete their entire lifecycle within one year setting seed that germinates freely. It is important to eradicate annual weeds when they are seedlings before they can reproduce.
   - Perennial weeds can survive year after year. They produce deeply penetrating tap roots, rhizomes or tubers for long-term survival. Many have the ability to regenerate from very small pieces of root. It is essential that no pieces are left behind when cultivating.
4. **Perennial Weeds:** Perennial weeds form a storage system in their roots or stems preserving for many years. They are very difficult to eradicate as they have a number of methods to ensure their survival: They may produce seed that may be dispersed to reach new ground as well as the surrounding area. Many can regenerate even if the top is removed by means of underground fleshy roots, rhizomes or bulbs. Perennials can survive through the winter by storing food in their roots or by storing food in stems and branches. It is essential to remove and destroy the underground fleshy roots, rhizomes and other storage organs to prevent re-growth of perennial weeds. Digging, tilling and mechanical cultivation often break up the roots of these weeds allowing them to survive and restore themselves. This is particularly true of those weeds with very deep roots. The most practical and effective form of control is to use systemic weed-killers. The plant absorbs the chemical and transports it through its entire system eventually killing the whole weed.
5. **Preventing Weeds:** The best way to control weeds is to prevent them from establishing in the garden. There are a number of ways to do this, which will reduce the need for weeding later.

(*a*) Clearing the Soil: Always clear the site of all annual and perennial weeds before planting. This may be done chemically or by hand. If the site is invaded with perennial weeds, treat the whole area with a weed-killer before planting season. Eradicate annual weeds by spraying or forking out before planting. It may be possible to treat soil invaded by perennial weeds by laying a carpet or light-excluding black polythene over the site. Then leave it undisturbed for at least two years. This can starve out perennial weeds.

(*b*) Keeping Plants Healthy: Strong and vigorous plants will be able to compete with weeds much more effectively than weak ones. Healthy plants forming a leafy canopy will discourage weeds from establishing beneath their spreading foliage.

(*c*) Mulching: A protective covering layer around plants blocks out light preventing weed seeds from germinating. Organic mulches need to be 10 cm (8 in) thick to be totally effective. Thinner layers (5 cm/2 in) may allow the occasional perennial weed to grow through but they are easy to remove. Avoid using garden compost or manure. This often contains weed seeds. Use only leaf mould, peat substitute or processed bark. Inorganic mulches are more effective at suppressing weed growth. A layer of black plastic sheeting will prevent annual weeds from establishing. Crops and other plants may be grown through the plastic sheeting by simply cutting a cross in the plastic and positioning desirable specimens through it. The unattractive plastic surface may be concealed with a layer of bark or gravel.

(*d*) Planting Ground Cover: There are a number of ground cover plants which will grow in dense carpets and suppress the germination of weed seeds. Plant them in weed-free soil to ensure good growth.

(*e*) Companion Planting: Some vegetable crops help to suppress or clear the ground of weeds. This needs to be done for a few seasons to exhaust the rhizomes. Potatoes compete well with annual weeds and may be grown to help retain weed-free ground for later planting.

(*f*) Controlling Weeds: Weeds may be controlled by manual, mechanical or chemical means. The choice of methods will usually depend of the type of weed and its location. Yearly weeds respond well to tilling, while perennial weeds need to be treated with weed-killer.

- **Manual Control of Weeds:** In many cases to control weeds in borders, vegetable gardens and small areas without harming neighbouring plants is by manual weeding. It may be either by hand or by using a hoe or a fork. Yearly weeds may be removed from the ground by hand-weeding or by shallow hoeing before they set seed. This should be done on a dry, sunny day, so that the weeds are easily loosened from the soil and dry out quickly. Use a sharp hoe with a back and forth sliding motion so that weeds become severed from the stems, preventing further development. Tilling will defeat most weeds and the reservoir of seeds in the soil layer will be exhausted if carried out regularly. Shallow rooting perennial weeds should be removed using a fork, so that the roots may be lifted intact. All of the rhizomes, roots or bulbils should be removed from the soil so that the weed does not have a chance to re-establish itself. Some perennials are particularly difficult to eradicate and may be resistant to many weed-killers. It may be necessary to control the growth of these weeds by repeatedly cutting down their foliage. Although new growth will regenerate quickly from their large food reserves, infestations can be considerably reduced in a few years. This technique is useful for perennials as regular mowing will finally weaken the plants.
- **Mechanical Control of Weeds:** Mechanical aids may be used against weeds. Rotavators (rotary cultivators) are suitable for dealing with yearly weeds in unplanted areas and between rows of vegetables. They should not be used where perennial

weeds are growing. They will chop the roots and distribute them across the area multiplying as new plants. A flame gun is a useful alternative to weed-killers. They may be used in areas such as paths and paving. Take extra care when using a weed burner so that nearby plants are not damaged.

- **Chemical Control of Weeds:** Weed-killers are the most effective solution for controlling weeds. They may be the only way of dealing with some persistent perennials. There are three major types of weed-killer application:
  1. Foliage activated: Applied by spray and enters the plant through its leaves or stem. Works by contact or systemic action.
  2. Soil activated: Applied to the soil, and enters the plant through its roots.
  3. Selective: Most kill broadleaved plants, but leave narrow-leaved grasses unharmed. Some leave ornamental plants while killing grassy weeds.

When working with weed-killers, it is essential to work carefully to minimise harm to the user or to the environment. Always wear protective clothing when mixing or applying chemicals, and never work in windy weather when there is a risk of spray being blown back or across to nearby plants. Also carefully follow the instructions for disposal of excess chemicals. They should not be poured down sinks, drains or watercourses. There are many ready-to-use weed-killers, which come with their own spray head attached. These are convenient to use. For larger areas it may be more economical to buy a concentrate to dilute later. Always read and follow the instructions on the packet when using weed-killers. While using chemicals to clear and replant an overgrown area, make a note of how much time is needed to leave the ground before replanting.

The best time of year to apply a systemic weed-killer is in late spring when the plant has started to grow and the plant's transport system is active. It is often worth cutting back large perennial weeds a few weeks before spraying. They produce healthy new foliage which will take in the weed-killer better. After applying weed-killer, it may take several weeks before the weed shows signs of dying. Re-apply the product if new growth appears, and then dig out and remove dead weeds.

E. Diseases

Plant diseases are caused by one of three organisms: bacteria, fungi or viruses. All groups may trouble from time to time, however bacterial and viral diseases are relatively rare. Diseases usually affect the growth or health of the plant visible by distortion, discoloration or wilting. It may ultimately lead to its death. Good garden hygiene is the key to disease prevention. Keeping the garden or greenhouse clear of decaying, diseased or dead material, trays, canes and other equipment at the end of each season can get rid of potential sources of infection. Choosing disease-resistant plant species will keep plants vigorous and healthy.

1. **Bacterial Diseases:** Many foliage plants are sensitive to bacterial diseases showing typical symptoms of leaf spots, blights, and wilting. Bacteria are found on the surface of all plant surfaces. Certain conditions such as high humidity, crowding and poor air circulation may lead them to multiply out of control. Misting plants also provide a film of water on the leaves where bacteria can multiply. Unhealthy plants often become weak making them prone to bacterial infection. To reduce plant weakness, avoid the following conditions:

- Too much, too little, or irregular watering.
- Fluctuating temperatures.

- Low light intensity.
- Poor soil drainage.
- Too large or too small a pot.
- A deficiency or an excess of nutrients.

The most severe diseases of foliage plants are caused by bacteria belonging to the genera Erwinia and Pseudomonas, which can cause infections such as fireblight and bacterial canker.

Fireblight is one of the most dangerous bacterial plant diseases. It may affect members of the rose family. The term 'fireblight' describes the appearance of the disease, which can make affected areas appear blackened, shrunken and cracked. Fireblight is caused by bacteria, which is produced from the cankers and spread by wind, rain, birds and insects. The first sign is the browning and withering of foliage. Oozing cankers appear on the branches, and the whole tree may eventually die within a few years. Infected areas should be removed by pruning. Any cuts are approximately 60 cm (2 ft) into healthy wood. Any pruning equipment should be disinfected between each cut. If the plant is small or the infection is severe, it is necessary to dig it up and destroy it.

Bacterial canker is a serious disease usually seen on plum and cherry trees. The leaves develop brown spots, which may be surrounded by a yellow halo. The spotted areas then fall out, giving a 'shot-hole' appearance. Lesions (cankers) begin to form on the bark and exude a sticky gum. Control may be carried out by pruning away the affected branches. Any pruning equipment should be thoroughly disinfected between each cut to reduce the risk of spreading the disease. The plants may also be sprayed with copper fungicide once a month.

2. **Fungal Diseases:** The most common diseases in the garden and greenhouse are caused by fungus. The most important are honey fungus, mildews and grey mould because they have many susceptible hosts.

3. **Viral Diseases:** All plants can be affected by viruses, which can cause a variety of symptoms depending on the disease. The leaves of infected plants may become yellow and distorted. The whole plant may show growth distortions such as stunting or abnormalities in flower formation. Viruses may spread horizontally between plants, by wind, insects or basic injury or vertically passed down from a parent plant. There is usually no cure for plant viruses, so prevention is the cure. Reduce the risk of horizontal transmission between plants by keeping tools and equipment clean. Greenhouse sap-sucking pests are a major carrier of viruses. Introduce suitable pest control measures to reduce their numbers. Always wash hands and tools after handling any suspect plants. Any plants badly infected by virus should be burned. Replacements should be planted in a new site in the garden. Always consider buying certified virus-free stock. These plants may be more expensive to buy, but they are more vigorous and worth any extra money.

F. Disorders

Plant disorder means nutritional deficiency or a physiological disorder. Unsuitable growing conditions such as too much or too little water or an inappropriate temperature range can also cause plants to show a range of symptoms like yellowing of foliage and wilting stems. Plants receiving unsatisfactory water, food, light or minerals will look unhealthy. They may not be able to resist attack from pests or diseases caused by bacteria, fungi or viruses.

Plants become unhealthy and vulnerable to pest and disease damage, if placed in unsuitable conditions. Plants should always be positioned in growing conditions suitable for their needs. Care should be taken that they get enough water, but not excessive water. They may also need to be protected during very hot weather to prevent scorching and in very cold weather to avoid damage by frost.

Nutrient deficiencies in plants are most commonly seen in light and free-draining soils. Foliage is most often affected becoming discoloured. Growth also usually becomes stunted. Nutrient deficiencies are relatively easy to treat.

1. **Chemical Damage:** Chemical damage to plants may arise in three major ways:

   (*a*) Careless application of a chemical.

   (*b*) Using the wrong chemicals for a particular problem.

   (*c*) Applying the right chemicals at the wrong rate or interval.

   Weed-killer damage can affect plants, which are unknowingly sprayed with weed-killer through careless application or by spray drift in windy conditions. Contamination may also occur if equipment used for weed-killer is used to water plants. Bleached patches appear on the affected foliage turning them brown. If the plant is severely contaminated, its growth may be affected leading to its death. Use a watering can instead of a sprayer and keep all equipment separately for use with weed-killers.

   Plants may also be damaged by fungicides or insecticides if they are applied at the wrong rate or during hot conditions. Never treat plants in bright sunlight. It may lead to scorching. Make sure that the manufacturer's guidelines for application rates are followed carefully. Young plants are more vulnerable to damage. They may be injured by the application of some chemical treatments.

2. **Mechanical Damage:** Mechanical damage involves injuries to plants from the careless use of garden machinery and tools. One of the most common forms is the removal of bark from trees by lawn mowers. Consider altering the shape of the lawn or have a wider area of longer grass around trees if this happens on a regular basis. Tree, shrub and other plants ties can cause choking. Point tight ties may be loosened by regular checks. One of the most serious forms of damage is from ragged and badly placed pruning cuts. This can provide entry points for disease weakening the plant. In severe cases they my lead to its death. Keep pruning equipment sharp. Make sure that any cuts are made in the right position.

EXERCISE

1. What methods are used to prevent pests and diseases to plants?
2. What is 'Organic Control' of plant management?
3. What is 'Biological Control' of plant management?
4. What is 'Chemical Control' of plant management?
5. What aspects should be taken into consideration for 'Plant Care'
6. Explain various plant diseases
7. What are the various types of "Plant disorders'?

9

Hard and Soft Landscape

A. Hard landscape

The basic integration in Landscape Design is to create spaces, sequence and furnishing the space. Spaces that are created are linked in sequence by route. Hard landscape elements are designed and built to fulfill the functions of landscape as well as enhancing it. The effect is spontaneous and quick. The floor and walls of an outdoor space includes pavement and walls comprised of concrete, masonry and raw materials like stone and gravel except plant material is considered 'Hardscape'.

The basic purpose of hard landscape is

- To cater needs not accommodated by soft landscape elements.
- To provide complimentary effect and to enhance the beauty of soft landscape.

These may be divided into the following categories based on the functions of the hardscape elements.

1. Separating elements
2. Special surfaces
3. Linkages
4. Furnishings

1. Separating Elements:

Physical and visual barriers control the movement of men, vehicles and animals. Indirectly, physical barrier functions as climate, sound and pollution control. Physical barriers are drainage ditch, moat, stream and steep embankment. Visual barriers are flower pots, solid wall and fences.

1. Planter box/Flower pots:

Planter box or Flower pots can be used where the soil is unsuitable for planting. They help in subdividing spaces into different areas. They can be arranged to show direction or access. They provide scale of surrounding landscape.

The design of Planter box or Flower pots is determined by the plant used and its surroundings. Drainage holes are essential. They may be placed where there is sufficient light, absorb noise, purify air or bad odour. They should not be placed making pedestrian route narrow. The material used should be cost-effective, easily available, vandal-proof and durable with aesthetic value.

Fig. 9.1. Planter box

Fig. 9.2. Paving

Fig. 9.3. Fence wall

2. Fence, Wall/Retaining Wall:

Fence, wall or retaining wall provides spaces or divided areas of ownership. It helps to block unpleasant view and odour. It gives security from intruders. It also prevents soil erosion.

Architectural image of fence, wall or retaining wall normally relates to design objectives, concept of landscape or existing building. Material which can be used should be easily available, water proof and durable.

2. Special Surfaces

Special surfaces are added features which indicate activities, event and safety like paving (gravel, cobbles, tarmac, bricks and pebbles) and pedestrian walkway.

1. Paving:

Paving indicates direction by using suitable, comfortable surfaces for pedestrian, compared to surfaces of other area. It also differentiates access to vehicles and pedestrian movement by using different surface finishes. At junctions or meeting points of pedestrians and vehicles, different material or levels can be adopted to indicate danger. Paving can be used as focal point for temporary stopping.

Paving material should be cost-effective and easy to maintain. It should be safe and sound. Rough finish prevents slipping. Soft material with rough finish could reduce and absorb noise sources.

Dark coloured surface finishes absorb light. The design pattern should make use of existing related pattern and arrangement. Scale and contrast can be used to differentiate various new patterns.

3. Linkages

Linkages or circulation systems are a combination of linear connectors/circulation paths, traffic generators and events along the connectors like entrances, bridges, steps and gateways.

Fig. 9.4. Bridge

1. Bridge:

Bridge links access from one place to another. It also helps to avoid dangerous or disturbing element and to provide aesthetic value to landscape design. It should be easy to use and safe to build, and located at suitable areas without causing damages.

The bridge design should consider safety and comfort as prime factors. The material should be durable, weatherproof and vandal proof. There should be an alternative route for users during maintenance to avoid mischief.

2. Steps:

Steps link areas of different levels and indicate access. Normally use uniform steps and avoid any design that can cause tiredness or discomfort with well-thought safety precautions. Landing should be provided for high staircases.

Fig. 9.5. Steps

Fig. 9.6. Seating

4. Furnishings

Structures that are added to spaces, to enhance and make complete the spaces like seating, dustbin, signage, lighting, sculptures and kiosk.

1. Seating:

Seating could attract and highlight some garden design. It can be used for relaxed viewing the surrounding or reading books or similar such activities. Seating design is normally based on the garden design concept.

Seating could be accommodated under big trees (large canopy/foliage) near covered buildings, next to a wall or plants sheltered from sunlight, and windy areas not obstructed by other landscape elements. Select places for seating having good and have pleasant views.

Comfort is the main criteria in design. Design should avoid intricate corners & spaces. Scale or size should be able to accommodate load as well as relate to the surrounding landscape scale. Materials used should be easily cleaned or painted. Structure of materials should be durable. Construction and maintenance costs should compliment the surrounding construction cost and landscape design. Modern or traditional materials can be chosen based on the context whether they are to be used in an urban or rural area.

2. Dustbin:

The dustbin should have easy access for garbage disposal and collection. There are different types of dustbins like wall mounted, free standing, removable, big sized where population is high. Dustbins are generally located near pedestrian access with other facilities such as toilets and recreation area, where people gathers, picnic or relax. They should not be located too close to each other to avoid bad odour or flies or bad view.

The design and material depends on location, method of collection, relationship to the surrounding landscape elements and capacity. Galvanized sheet metal, aluminium, timber, fibre-glass and concrete are normally used for dustbins.

Fig. 9.7. Dustbin

Fig. 9.8. Signage

3. Signage:

All signage should have standardised design, colour and lettering. It should be located at an appropriate place. It should of suitable size to convey information. Signage should not obstruct aesthetic value of other elements. Type of information normally conveyed through signage is: preventive, prohibitive, warning and general. The material used depends on cost, design, durability and maintenance.

4. Lighting:

Lighting is meant to illuminate dark and insecure areas. It also illuminates and enhances a focal element or dangerous objects. It provides suitable mood for occasions. There may be three types of lighting.

(*a*) Roads and highways lighting

(*b*) Pedestrians lighting

(*c*) Decorative lighting

Safety and comfort are prime factors in choosing a material for lighting. The lighting material should be durable, weatherproof and vandal proof. Its maintenance should be safe and easy.

Fig. 9.9 Lighting

5. Sculptures:

Carvings and sculptures act as an attraction conforming to the design concept. They also indicate owner's wealth. As a principle avoid using symbols or forms which offend culture, religion or the owner. It should be placed at safe and strategic place relating to the scale of park or garden

The design or material should be related to the concept of the park or garden like modern, abstract, classic or traditional. The material used should be durable and aesthetic. Most commonly used materials are concrete, aluminum, fiber glass, timber, glass or perspex.

6. Kiosk:

A shelter or kiosk is normally meant for relaxing and gathering, as a viewing place, as an attraction or as a node or focal point. It should be located in a secure and pleasant place having a nice view.

The architecture or image of a shelter or kiosk is normally related to existing landscape, building design, national identity or situation. The material should be weatherproof and easily available to construct.

B. Soft landscape

There are three basic aspects that soft landscaping include, namely plantation, turfing and water features. All these features are required to complete a thriving garden.

1. **Plantation:** The plantation process involves the planning and assessment of the garden design. Preparation of the surface area, planting the shrubs, trees and identifying the various plant

Fig. 9.10. Plantation

breeds are keys to ensure a balanced and compatible garden environment. The finishing layer is done with the use of pebbles, stones, wood chips and many other materials, which can be chosen.

2. **Turfing:** This process involves the grass being cut into various patterns to adorn the garden. At the same time identification of various plant breeds is done through turfing.
3. **Water features:** Strategically placed water fountains and waterfalls improve the garden atmosphere. Flowing water fountains and waterfalls enrich the garden and create a vivid atmosphere. Various garden ponds, lagoons and small pools can be built right into the garden. The water also brings in moisture, which in turn attracts birds and small wildlife.

Fig. 9.11. Turfing

Fig. 9.12. Water features

Properly designed and constructed soft landscape treatments such as shrub beds, tree planting and grassing can create interesting and dynamic public spaces. Their design and construction should be carefully considered to ensure that they serve their intended purposes like

1. Providing safe and accessible public spaces with solar screening around buildings.
2. Give distinct landscape character for recreational areas directing the flow of pedestrian and vehicular traffic along paths and roadways.
3. Providing habitat for wildlife and reduce noise giving privacy for properties.
4. Creating interest and visual stimulation in public spaces.
5. Defining boundaries between two or more facilities and screening of undesirable objects.

When designing soft landscape for public spaces the following principles help improve public safety:

1. Locate trees maintaining minimum clearance requirements from services and sight lines in harmony with existing or proposed buildings.
2. Do not use shrubs with sharp or spiky foliage, where they may cause injuries, such as pathways and playgrounds.

3. Make sure that planting does not restrict or interfere with access and allow movement of the disabled.

C. Important aspects of "Hard landscape' and 'Soft landscape' in landscape design

1. Design to reduce maintenance:

There is no maintenance-free landscape. However, proper planning can keep maintenance to minimum. The following guidelines seek to do this.

1. Keep grass areas large enough to guide mowing equipment.
2. Provide adequate surface drainage to shrub beds and grass areas.
3. Mowing around trees in lawn areas should not be blocked. A mowing edge should be constructed against walls and planting beds to avoid hand clipping. Edges should be flushed with adjacent grass areas.
4. Plant trees and shrubs in masses and in beds with a minimum 75–100 mm depth of mulch.
5. Choose sturdy plants of long life requiring minimal maintenance.
6. Design paths and paving to accommodate desire lines.
7. Allow for adequate preparation of soil for planting and grassing.

2. Soil selection and protection:

Soil selection for plants is an important factor when designing for soft landscape elements. In many cases, the existing soil cannot provide trees and shrubs with sufficient nutrients and water penetration for survival. In such cases soil needs to be imported to supplement the existing site soil. For large or environmentally sensitive sites where importing soil is not an option, soil tests may indicate the most effective way to improve the soil. The simplest and most effective protection for trees is fencing out construction activity. Maintenance access to each tree must be considered at the design stage. Feeder roots of trees grow in the top 150–300 mm of the soil. This feeder zone can extend two to seven times the diameter of the canopy drip line. Major structural roots may penetrate to depths of 1–5 meters. No site sheds, building materials or vehicles are to be placed within the drip zone of existing trees. The drip zone should be fenced off, and all trees must be protected from compaction within the feeder zone.

3. Porous paving:

Porous paving is useful where a hard surface is required to be installed near trees. Using structural soils and porous paving together allow water to filter through the paving surface to the soil layers below providing water and nutrients to the plant's root system. Adequate drainage must be installed with permeable paving.

4. Root barriers:

Root barriers can provide protection to the surrounding infrastructure against disruption from tree roots with minimal impact on the tree. Properly installed root barriers can protect pavement, footings and kerbs from cracking and lifting. Root barriers should be installed vertically in a continuous length in a narrow trench with the top edge flush with the finished ground surface. The trench should be backfilled and tamped sufficiently to avoid later caving. The barrier should not be torn or pierced.

5. Mulching materials:

Mulching material for planting areas should be selected on the basis of its general purpose and location of the bed within the environment. The settled depth should be 75–100 mm, when applying mulch to newly constructed shrub beds. This will prevent most seed germination in the soil. Fine mulch should not be used, as it is prone to decompose or washed away rapidly.

6. General design considerations:

During the design process, information on all established trees should be recorded showing species type, height, canopy spread and trunk circumference and location. When established trees are designated for keeping in development areas the canopy, trunk and roots must be protected from damage. A decision to retain, prune or remove trees should be made at the early design stage with full recognition of their value, potential costs, advantages and disadvantages, and alternative design strategies available to retain the trees. If damage to the roots is likely to kill a tree then removing the tree before work starts will avoid the difficulty of later removal. In any condition keeping of large trees in confined areas such as courtyards should be carefully considered in view of the public safety and maintenance implications. Any excavation or level build-up around trees must be minimised. Where level build-up is necessary, the fill soil should be the same texture as the original surface soil otherwise downward capillary water flow may be affected. If the ground is heavily compacted some aeration should be provided before the fill soil is added.

EXERCISE

1. What is the difference between 'Hard landscape' and 'Soft landscape' in Landscape Design?
2. What is 'Hard landscape'? Describe with examples.
3. What is 'Soft landscape'? Describe with examples.
4. What are the important aspects to be taken into consideration for "Hardscape' and 'Softsape' in landscape design?

10

Landscape Construction

Planting a lawn, filling flower beds and designing walkways comprise only half the landscape design work. Today's landscape designer should also take into consideration issues like sustainability, drainage, shape, pests and diseases harmful to trees, shrubs and flowers.

Landscape construction roots can be traced to the early public parks in Europe and Great Britain. Parks were popular places for carriage rides, leisurely strolls and courtship rituals. They need to be induced with a sense of culture and civilization maintaining the unspoiled beauty of nature. It involved defining broad paths for horses and pedestrians, constructing bridges over streams, clearing unsightly rocks and dead trees and providing benches and shelters for people. Wealthy people had servants to tend to their private gardens. In rural areas people planted only vegetation which could be harvested and sold. The advent of residential suburbs made homeowners have front and backyards for landscaping.

There are broadly three types of landscape construction.

1. Residential properties meant to be lived in by individuals and families. They may be bungalows, huge mansions or housing complexes.
2. Commercial facilities such as office buildings, restaurants, shopping malls, amusement parks, golf courses and stores.
3. Environmental design projects like a botanical garden.

Landscape designers need to be sensitive regarding the use of plants for low maintenance and low water, irrigation designed for maximum efficiency and minimal waste, materials from recycled, renewable or sustainable resources, and projects approached in an environmentally conscientious manner to create beautiful landscape.

Site clearing is the first step in preparing the site for new construction. It covers vegetation removal and structural demolition. All organic matter must be cleared from the construction so that sub-grades may be properly prepared. Topsoil is typically stripped to a depth of 10-15 cm (4"-6") and stocked for later use for plants and embankment stabilizing grasses.

A. Earthwork

After a site has been cleared and stripped of its organic soil, it is prepared for general excavation. Typically, top and bottom of slope grade stakes are set to indicate to operators where embankment cuts and fills begin and end. Remove intended trees and other types of vegetation from an area to be graded. In some cases, all existing plant material should be chopped and mixed with topsoil. This technique often proves to be an excellent way to restore a similar type of vegetative cover. Sod should be removed or broken up to prevent lumping during reuse. Earthwork operations are divided into cut, fill, trenching and bulk excavation. Earth is moved to create platforms for new construction of all roads, buildings, parking and lawns. Sub-grades are generally set before trench or bulk basement excavation. Work is scheduled to avoid long delays or multiple handling.

1. Cut Operations:

Cut operations lower the sub-grade. It may be prepared to receive topsoil for planted areas. Scrapers may be used to shape embankments for large areas and bulldozers for deep cuts. Cut slopes may rest at 1:2 in most soils, but a 1:3 or 1:4 slopes is more stable and needs less maintenance cost. Long slopes may need bench terracing for stability. The area surrounding the proposed building site is graded to rough sub-grade before footing excavation to minimise the cost of excessive trenching or bulk excavation. Well points or curtain drains may be needed to lower the water table during construction. Test pits and borings during early exploration indicate the presence of ground water.

2. Pipe and Pit Trenching:

A backhoe is normally used for trenching of utilities. It has a normal reach of 180 cm (6 ft). Extensive or heavy duty trenching may employ a larger power hoe of 240·300 cm (8-10 ft) reach, or a wheel or chain trencher. Chain trenchers have an excavation capacity of 38-380 ml (50-500 cubic yards) per hour; depending on model type. Large trenches require slip-form bracing to prevent trench wall collapse. They are backfilled immediately after each pipe segment is laid. Basin structure pits are usually dug during this operation.

B. Fill Operations

Cutting and filling can be conducted simultaneously. The fill portion must be compacted to predetermined construction standards. Fill for planted areas should be compacted to retain 30 percent minimum porosity. Fill material must be put down in 150-200 mm (6-8 in) layers. Compact and test each layer to conform to specified densities. Topsoil is added at the end to bring the grades to the levels and slopes shown on the grading plans. All surface areas intended to fill are normally roughened to create a mechanical bond between the sub-grade and the new fill. Fill is systematically placed in specified layers or lifts (15-30 cm or 6-12 in.) and compacted by proper machinery. Scrapers may place the soil in accurate lifts by setting discharge rate and bin blade height. They are the most economical method for executing large area fills. Trucks deposit piles which need spreading by bulldozer to the specified lift depth. This method is typical for light to medium construction. Each lift must be compacted to achieve the specified density of 95%. This will match rate of infiltration and bearing capacity of undisturbed earth. This operation is also called "controlled fill placement" and is repeated until the new sub-grade elevation is achieved. Soil types determine the method used for compaction

1. General Fill:

General fill is usually subsoil taken from on-site cut and should be structurally suited to avoid differential settlement or excessive swelling. Good site design balances cut and fill and avoids sites with unsuitable construction soils.

2. Trench and Foundation Backfill:

Backfilling of pipe and foundation trenches requires controlled lifts and careful compaction to avoid differential settlement and trench wall slump. Sands for pipe and aggregates for perforated drain are used as bedding. Backfill material should contain graduated particle sizes, but should not contain Iarge stones, which may create air pockets.

3. Structural Fill:

Structural fill is placed under building floor slabs. It needs very strict placement and compaction. It consists of graded aggregate base material placed In 15 cm (6 in) lifts, and vibrated and rolled to achieve 95% density. Such structural fills should not exceed 90 cm (3 ft) in normal circumstances for cost and stability,

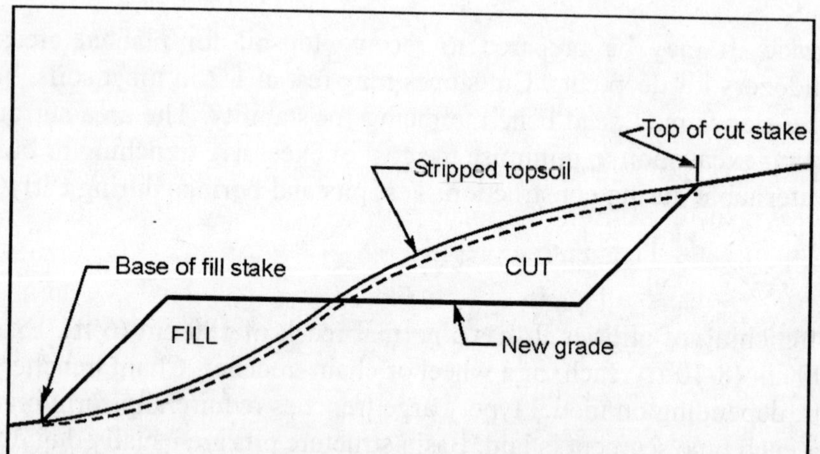

Fig. 10.1. Cut and Fill of land

C. Drainage and Utilities

Placement of sanitary and storm sewer basins and pipes begin after cut and fill operations are completed. Thus it helps to connect outfalls to subsequent building drains, site curtain drains, and other temporary dewatering and construction runoff filtering systems. Newly buried pipes should have sufficient soil cover in areas subject to heavy vehicular traffic. Most thin wall (steel and polymer) pipes require 75 cm (30 in) of soil cover to prevent crushing. At this stage of construction, sub-grades may be 30-45 cm (12-18 in) below finish grades, All drain basins require controlled backfills to prevent lateral shifting in vehicular pavements. Most basin pits are dug with a power hoe.

D. Grading

Grading operations prepare the site to receive pavements, plantings and all other site improvements. The site is surveyed to set finish layout and grading stakes. Stakes are offset from road centerlines and pavement edges to avoid interference with subsequent construction operations. Grade stakes are normally offset 30-60 cm (2-3 ft) from proposed pavement edges. There are many types of equipment that can be used to do grading.

In case of grading rocks, the initial site design and the ultimate grading plan should be prepared based upon the knowledge of the composition and other characteristics of the soil and rock to be moved. Rock is generally considered to be any material which requires blasting before it can be dug or moved by machines. The cost of blasting and moving rock is 7 to 10 times higher than moving cohesive soil.

The most useful data in preparing a grading plan of rock is

- the depth of soil cover to rock,
- amount of easily breakable top layer of rock,
- amount of rock to be blasted,
- type of rock .

Rock is typically classified into three major groups.

1. **Igneous:** Igneous rock is solidified from a molten state, either at or beneath the surface of the earth. It is crystalline. Typically it does not exhibit a grain. It breaks irregularly depending on its composition.
2. **Sedimentary:** Sedimentary rock is made from the sedimentation of soil, plant and animal remains. Rock hardened as a result of pressure, time and the deposition of natural cements at ocean depths. It will fracture along the planes of sedimentation
3. **Metamorphic:** Metamorphic rock consists of previously igneous or sedimentary rock. Rock was altered by extreme heat and pressure at great depths or along tectonic fault lines. It often exhibits some staining or foliation. Rock may fracture naturally or during blasting and excavation.

When soil or rock is dug or blasted out of its original position, it breaks into particles or chunks. This creates more space and adds to its mass. This increase in volume is called swell. When soil is placed in a new location with nominal compaction, these voids are filled and some shrinkage occurs. Compaction will not compress rock excavation to its original volume because rock swells. Grading involves two phases: rough grading and finish grading.

1. Rough Grading:

Rough grading is necessary after all cut and fill operations have established approximate elevations for proposed sub-grades. Bulldozers, road graders and hand labor are needed to precisely set edges and create uniform slopes. Grading under slabs and pavement structures requires precision within 1.5 cm (1/2 in).

2. Finish Grading:

Finish grading is the final placement of topsoil between pavements and structure. Soil depths may vary by planting type. This is completed after major planting of trees and all other activities.

E. Grading criteria

Grading becomes an integral part of the design process on par with the location of buildings, circulation planning and use of all landscape qualities. In many cases the grading scheme is a primary determinant in the total design. Grading may be done for a number of functional and aesthetic reasons.

Abbreviations on Grading Plans

Table 10.1. Abbreviations on Grading Plans

No	*Abbreviation*	*Meaning*	*No*	*Abbreviation*	*Meaning*
1.	CI	Contour interval	9.	IE	Invert elevation
2.	TC	Top of curb	10.	RE	Rim elevation
3.	BC	Bottom of curb	11.	DI	Drain inlet
4.	TW	Top of wall	12.	SD	Storm drain
5.	BW	Bottom of wall	13.	MH	Man hole
6.	HP	High point	14.	CB	Catch basin
7.	LP	Low point	15.	PL	Property line
8.	TS	Top of steps	16.	ROW	Right of way

F. Methods of Expressing Slope

Slope is expressed in terms of a percentage, proportion or degree.

1. As percentage:

Percentage of slope is expressed in the number of meters rise in 100 m. of horizontal distance. It is referred as rise/run. For example, if the slope rises 2 m. in 100 m, it is considered a 2 percent slope. The percentage of slope can be calculated by the following formula:

$$G = D/L \times 100$$

G = gradient in percentage

D = vertical rise

L = horizontal distance

2. As proportion:

Slope can also be expressed as a ratio of the horizontal distance to the vertical rise like two to one (2:1). The ratio method is normally used for steeper slopes like 4:1 (25%).

3. As Degree:

Slope is expressed in degrees only on large scale earth moving projects like strip-mining and other extractive operations.

4. Spot Elevations:

Spot elevations are used to establish limits of slope, to locale contour lines and to provide detail for establishing control points, which cannot be obtained by contour lines. The elevation of any point on an accurately drawn contour plan may be determined by interpolation.

G. Making a Contour Map

Contour lines show the height above sea level (in meters). Most maps have contour lines every 10 m. Contour lines evenly spaced and wide apart indicate a uniform and gentle slope. Contour lines evenly spaced and close together indicate a uniform and steep slope. The closer the contour lines are to each other, the steeper the slope.

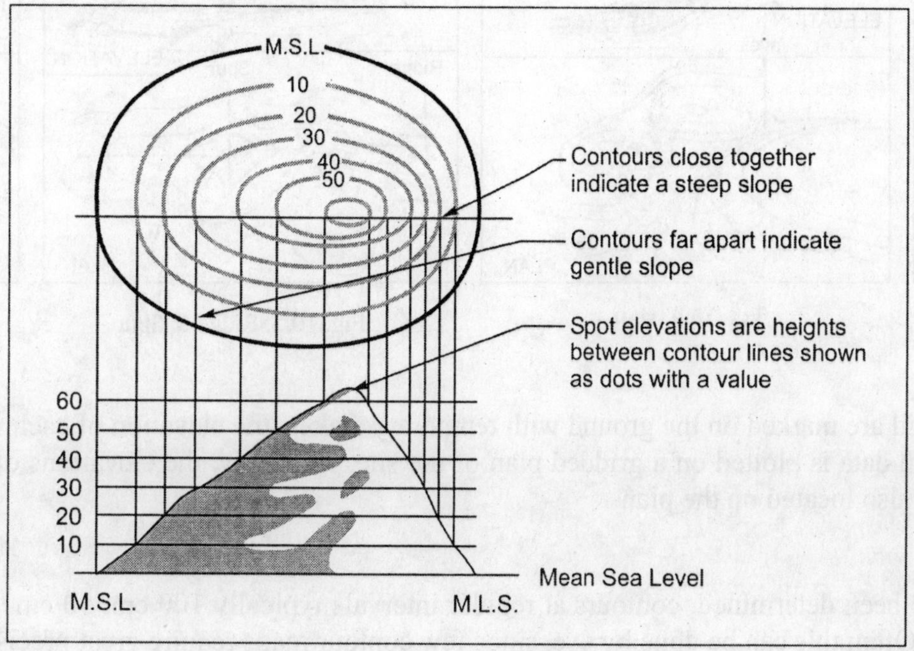

Fig. 10.2. Contour diagram

Terms normally used in a contour map are given below:

- **Hill top:** This is a point or small area of high ground. Here the ground slopes down in all directions.
- **Valley:** Contours indicating a valley are U-shaped and tend to parallel a major stream before crossing it. The more gradual the fall of a stream, the farther each contour parallels it. The curve of the contour crossing always points upstream.
- **Ridge:** A ridge is a line of high ground with minor variations along its crest. All points of the ridge crest are higher than the ground on both sides of the ridge.
- **Spur:** A spur is a short, continuously sloping line of higher ground normally jutting out from the side of a ridge.
- **Saddle:** A saddle is a dip or low point along the crest of a ridge.

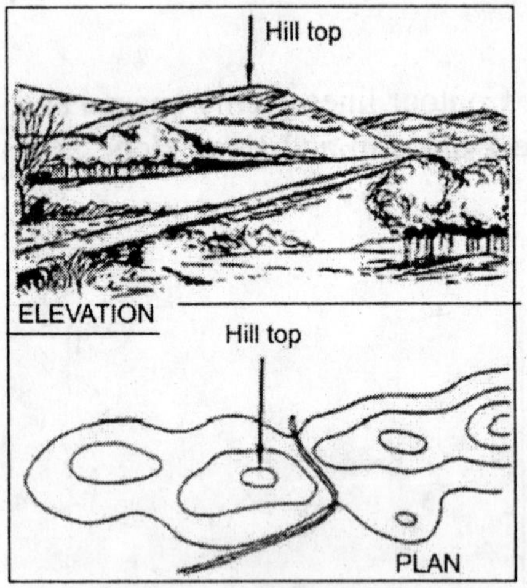

Fig. 10.3. Hill top

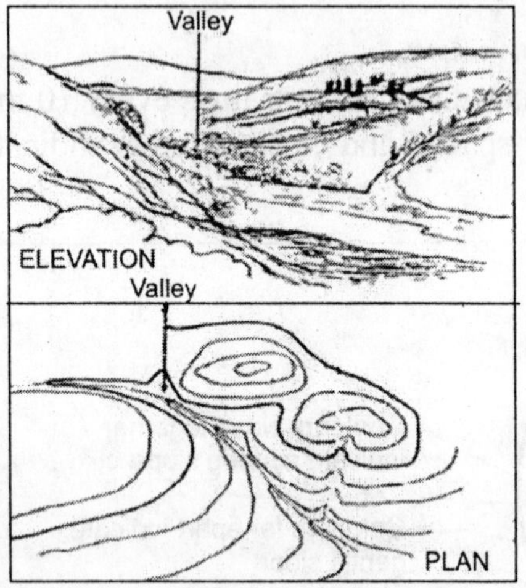

Fig. 10.4. Valley

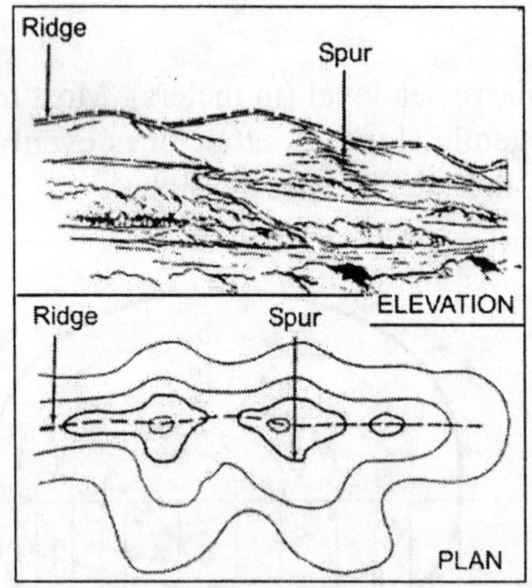

Fig. 10.5. Ridge & Spur

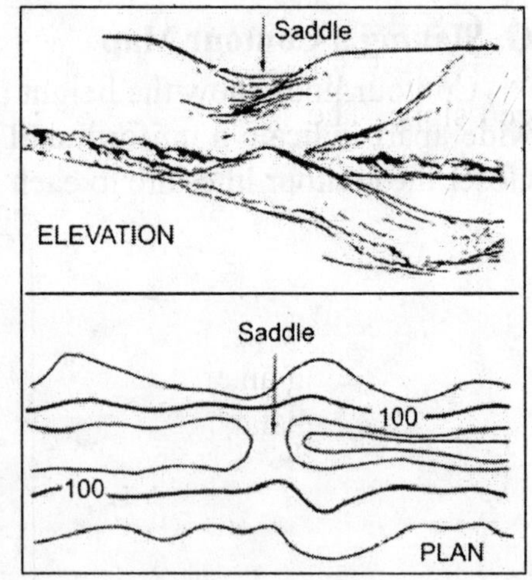

Fig. 10.6. Saddle

1. Field Survey:

All intersection points of a grid are marked on the ground with temporary stakes. the elevation of each intersection point are taken with a transit or level and the elevation data is plotted on a gridded plan of the site. Normally, the elevations of critical high or low points that fall between the intersections are also located on the plan.

2. Plotting Contours:

Once all spot elevations have been determined, contours at regular intervals typically 100 cm, 50 cm. or 25 cm (5 ft. 2 fl, or 1 ft) can be located and plotted on a map. Often this can be done by eye, since few contour maps require great precision.

3. Preparing a Site Grading Plan:

Grading of a site should be thought of as a systematic process that begins with the analysis and understanding of the existing site and ends with an overall detailed grading plan.

4. Site Analysis:

Study the general lay of the land by using topographic maps and site visits.

1. Determine high points, low points, ridges and valleys.
2. Note the natural drainage systems and direction of flow, which exists on the site.

5. Site Use Concept:

Determine how existing landform would affect proposed use areas, such building locations, roads, parking areas, walkways, plazas and lawn areas.

6. Schematic Grading Plan:

Define general use areas, set building floor areas by spot elevations, and draw drainage flow using slope arrows pointing along the direction of flow. This will help in the following procedures:

1. Developing a general landform concept.
2. Locating swales and surface water flow.
3. Locating drainage containers.
4. Calculating water runoff for various areas.
5. Defining an area that could be altered (raised or lowered) with limited impact on drainage or existing trees. This area could be used to help balance any surplus cut or fill.

7. Grading by Spot Elevations:

Grade by spot elevations and form preliminary contouring, using the following steps in the order shown. Always strive to keep disturbed areas as small as possible.

1. Set tentative gradients and spot grades on roads, walkways and swales. Establish critical spot elevations.
2. Set the building grade circuit *i.e.,* floor elevation, stops, walls, terraces etc
3. Draw in preliminary contours at 1.5 m or 3 m (5 or 10 ft) intervals depending upon the scale of the project and topographic change. Make certain that all gradients and slopes are within the maximum/minimum criteria for a particular use.
4. Complete all contour alterations within the property line or project limits.

8. Final Grading Plan:

1. Prepare final road profiles.
2. Indicate changes in direction or rate of slopes.
3. Show spot elevations for all critical points, including manholes, inverts, drainage structures, tops and bottoms of all walls, steps, and curbs at intersections and/or other critical points.
4. Draw proposed contours and complete the final grading plan.
5. Complete an estimate of the amount of cut and fill based on the proposed grading plan, and, adjust the amount of one or both to make them balance.

9. Recommended Gradients:

Grading of outdoor areas is aimed at controlling surface storm water runoff while providing safe and efficient pedestrian and vehicular movement. Essentially all surfaces should have some slope or pitch for proper drainage.

10. Earth Fill against Buildings:

Earth fill against buildings may be desirable for insulation or aesthetic reasons. It is important to note that soil and related moisture may cause decay and promote the growth of insects damaging or destroying some of the materials used in the construction of the building. The exterior surfacing and structural system of a building determine the height to which fill may be brought up against a structure.

H. Roadways

1. Grading and Alignment:

The principles and criteria for the design of major urban and rural highways are determined by the concerned authorities. The standards for streets and local access roads in residential, institutional, commercial and industrial areas are determined by local standards. Roadway design consists of two major phases.

1. Alignment of the road-giving it horizontal and vertical direction.
2. Grading the adjacent landscape to the road edge.

The designer of a roadway should go beyond merely satisfying the engineering requirements and see the user as an active player in the landscape.

The following criteria should be considered during the grading phase of the roadway

1. Remove extra soil to expose potential vistas.
2. Use roadside mounds to screen undesirable views.
3. Improve the soil adjacent to a road to enhance the growth of plants.
4. Blend the new slopes with the existing terrain.

2. Swales and Ditches:

Typically, swales are shallow, have a parabolic cross section, and are very wide, while ditches are deeper and have a narrower geometric configuration.

Storm water management swales are commonly used in grading to move water gently from one part of the site to another. Their function is to collect and divert the flow of surface runoff away from critical parts of a site At their terminus, swales must either spread the channelized water into sheet drainage or empty the water into a ditch, stream or underground drainage system.

The slope of the channel determines the velocity of flow and consequently the erosive potential. Since the side slopes of the swale do not affect this rate of flow, they may be much steeper and respond to other design criteria.

3. Existing Trees:

Grading around existing trees should be managed with great care, using one or more of the following techniques:

1. Avoid grading, cutting or filling above the root zone of a tree. For most species it means staying outside the drip line of the tree. The weight of the grading equipment driven over the root zone will tear foot hairs and compact the soil, thereby restricting vital water and air from flowing to and being assimilated by the roots.
2. If filling around an existing tree cannot be avoided, then the tree must be protected. This technique permits adequate flow of air and water to the roots of the tree.
3. In another way a deck is constructed, with footings which do not disturb the root system around tree. The deck's layout can be

adjusted to the specific site conditions. When buildings or other such structures are involved, it is better to use lightweight footings with crawl spaces rather than on-grade slabs with compacted sub-grades.

I. Erosion Control by Grading

Most erosion is caused by flowing water. The size and shape of a watershed, the porosity of its soils, and the length and gradient of its slopes and channels are key determinants. They control the volume and velocity of runoff and the risk of erosion. Several site grading techniques can be employed to limit the size, shape, length and gradient of these slopes. Gradients can be reduced by extending the length of a slope. This uses more land but reduces the amount of erosion and slumping of hillsides. Diversion swales, ditches and dikes can intercept and divert runoff from the face of a slope.

J. Parking Areas

In grading of parking areas, the minimum and maximum gradients required for vehicular access and parking areas are often the major determinants for the grading plan of a site. The recommended maximum cross slope for a parking area is 10 percent. The steeper transitional area between bays can be taken up by a planting bay and a ramp. In extreme circumstances single-loaded parking bays may be used to fit steep slopes. Similarly, a combination of ramps and segmented parking bays may be used to achieve a grading solution on a slope with existing vegetation.

K. Estimating earthwork

Techniques for estimating earthwork quantities are only approximate. Three methods are normally used to prepare estimates of the quantities of grading needed. They are Grid or Borrow Pit Method, Average End-Area Method and Contour Method. Contour Method is commonly used by landscape architects because it is very accurate for making final grading adjustments and for preparing cost estimates.

EXERCISE

1. What are various 'Earthwork' operations?
2. What are various 'Fill' Operations?
3. Explain 'Grading' of site.
4. What are the various methods of expressing 'slope'?
5. How do you make a 'Contour map'?
6. How 'Roadways' are formed?
7. Write short notes on the following:
   (*a*) Drainage and Utilities
   (*b*) Erosion Control
   (*c*) Vehicle Parking
   (*d*) Estimating earthwork

11

Landscape Design Code

The requirements of landscape planning and design to promote quality of outdoor built environment and protection of land and its resources as per National Building Code 2005 of India is given below:

A. Terminology

- **Avenue:** A wide road or pathway lined with trees on either sides.
- **Buffer:** The use of landscape to curtail view, sound or dust with plants or earth berms, wall, or any such element.
- **Climber:** (Creeper/Vine): A non-supporting plant, woody or herbaceous, which clings to a wall, trellis or other structures as it grows upward.
- **Columnar:** A slender, upright plant form.
- **Contour:** The form of the land, existing or proposed; a part of the topography, indicated by map lines at intervals as desired, to understand the landform clearly. The contour line though imaginary, indicates continuous elevation above mean sea level or an assumed datum line.
- **Contour Interval:** The difference in elevation or the vertical distance measured between consecutive contour lines.
- **Deciduous Tree:** Tree that sheds all its leaves in autumn or in dry season.
- **Egress:** A way out, or exit.
- **Elevation:** A contour line or notation of relative altitude, useful in plotting existing or proposed feature.
- **Evergreen Tree:** Tree that remains green for most part of the year and sheds leaves slowly throughout the year.
- **Exotic:** A plant that is not native to the area in which it is planted.
- **Fencing:** A barrier of plant or construction material used to set off the boundary of an area and to restrict visual or physical passage in or out of it.
- **Finished Grade:** Grade accomplished after landscape features are installed and completed as shown on plan, as proposed contours.

- **Foliage:** The collective leaves of a plant or plants.
- **Geo-textile:** Any permeable textile (natural or synthetic) used with foundation, soil, rock, earth or any other geotechnical engineering-related material as an integral part of a human made project, structure or
- **Grade:** The slope or lay of the land as indicated by a related series of elevations.
- **Gradient:** The degree of slope of a pipe invert or road or land surface. The gradient is a measure of the slope height as related to its base. The slope is expressed in terms of percentage or ratio.
- **Grading:** The cutting and/or filling of earth to establish smooth finish contours for a landscape construction project. Grading facilitates good drainage and sculpts land to suit the intent of landscape design.
- **Grasses:** Plants that characteristically have joint stems, sheaths and narrow blades (leaves).
- **Groundcover:** The planting material that forms a carpet of low height; these low-growing plants are usually installed as the final part of landscape construction.
- **Hard Landscape:** Civil work component of landscape architecture such as pavement, walkways, roads, retaining walls, sculpture, street amenities, fountains and other built environment.
- **Hardy Plant:** Plants that can withstand harsh temperature variations, pollution, dust, extreme soil conditions, and minimal water requirements and the likes. These plants have ability to remain dormant in such conditions and survive.
- **Hedge:** Number of shrubs or trees (often similar species) planted closely together in a line. A hedge may be pruned to shape or allowed to grow to assume its natural shape.
- **Herb:** An annual plant with a non-woody or fleshy structure. Certain herbs are highly useful for cooking or of high medicinal value.
- **Ingress:** A way in, or entrance.
- **Invert:** The low inside point of a pipe, culvert, or channel.
- **Kerb:** A concrete or stone edging along a pathway or road often constructed with a channel to guide the flow of storm water and thereby serving dual purpose.
- **Mound:** A small hill or bank of earth, developed as a characteristic feature in landscape.
- **Native:** A plant indigenous to a particular locale.
- **Natural Grade:** Grade consisting of contours of unmodified natural landform.
- **Screen:** A vegetative or constructed hedge or fence used to block wind, undesirable views, noise, glare and the like, as part of landscape design; also known as 'screen planting' and 'buffer plantation'.
- **Sediment:** The product of erosion processes; the solid material, both mineral and organic, that is in suspension, is being transported or has been moved from its site of origin by air, water, gravity or ice.
- **Shrub:** A woody plant of low to medium height, deciduous or evergreen, generally has many stem.
- **Soft Landscape:** The natural elements in landscape design, such as plant materials and the soil itself.

- **Spot Elevation:** In surveying and contour layout, an existing or proposed elevation noted as a dot on the plan.
- **Street/Outdoor Furniture:** Items of furnishing in outdoor landscape.
- **Swale:** A linear wide and shallow depression used to temporarily store, route or filter runoff. A swale may be grassed or lined.
- **Topsoil:** The uppermost layer of the soil.
- **Transplanting:** Moving a plant from its place of origin to another location.
- **Tree:** A woody plant, generally taller than 2.00 m, with a well-distinguished trunk or trunks below the leaf crown.
- **Tree Grate:** A metal grille, installed at the base of a tree otherwise surrounded by pavement, which allows the free passage of air, water, and nutrients to the tree root, but does not interfere with the foot traffic.
- **Tree/Plant Guard:** The protection constructed around a tree to deter vandalism and helps to prevent damage. It could be made of metal, bamboo or concrete or the like.

B. Permit

1. Application for License or Permit and Required Drawings:

Any development project for which a permit or license is required, shall make application to the Authority on the prescribed form containing such particulars as the Authority may require. The form shall be signed by the owner and shall include required information.

2. Site Plan:

The site plan to be submitted with the application for permit shall be drawn to a scale of not less than 1 in 500 for a site up to ten hectares and not less than 1 in 1000 for site more than 10 hectares. The following information shall be provided in addition to requirements for Site Plan.

1. Existing and proposed topographic contours at interval not exceeding 50 cm and/or spot elevations as pertinent and Bench Mark of site with reference to the City Datum relative to the Mean Sea Level.
2. Limits of the 100 year flood plain and water surface elevation (when applicable).
3. Location of existing major physical features, such as railway track, drainage ways etc.
4. Location of service utilities adjacent to the project with relevant top and invert levels clearly indicated.
5. Point of egress and ingress including locations and width of road.
6. Fully dimensioned loading spaces and maneuvering areas.
7. Parking including, location, parking spaces, size and number, and typical parking space details for both handicapped and standard spaces.
8. Vehicular, bicycle, pedestrian and handicapped circulation clearly identified.
9. Detail for parking areas including type of lighting, material for paving, and security rooms, rest rooms; and type of directional signage etc.
10. Drainage system, proposed finish ground elevations and finish grades.

11. Location of proposed fire hydrant points.
12. Location and dimension of fire lanes.
13. Proposed lighting layout.
14. Landscape irrigation points and source of water.
15. Fences, walls, or vegetation for screening by type, material, height, location, and spacing.
16. Location of proposed street furniture.
17. Refuse container location, size, and access.
18. Landscape paving materials with location.
19. Location, type, size, and height of existing and proposed signage.
20. List of existing trees with botanical and common names and height of the tree
21. Prior approvals.

C. Landscape Plan Contents and Specifications

Landscape plan and drawings shall consist of the plans and details as given below

1. Grading Plan:

The grading plan to be submitted with the application for permit shall be drawn to a scale of not less than 1 in 500 for a site up to 10 hectares and not less than 1 in 1000 for site more than 10 hectares. The grading plan will include measures for soil and sedimentation control and also measures during construction to prevent soil erosion, and also water harvesting practices.

2. Planting Plan:

The planting plan shall be drawn to a scale of not less than 1 in 200 for a site up to ten hectares and not less than 1 in 500 for site more than 10 hectares with part plans at 1 in 200 of two of the design areas. Planting plan should include plant material schedule. The planting plan and landscape plan must show identical information to avoid conflict between both plans. The planting plan shall include the following layouts drawn to the scale:

1. Location of proposed trees, shrubs, ground covers and lawn area indicated clearly with appropriate symbols and legend.
2. The size of plant material indicated in the drawing should be shown as diameter of canopy for tree and spread for shrubs and ground cover. Two years growth will be considered as full maturity size for shrubs and ground covers and ten years growth will be considered for trees.
3. The Botanical name could be indicated as a symbol on the main drawing (for example *Deionix regia* as *Dr)*. Plant names should be tabulated in alphabetical order under heads Trees, Shrubs, Groundcovers, Climbers and Grass.
4. Functional attributes and growth pattern tabulation to be attached.
5. All existing vegetation shall be marked on the landscape plan and areas designated for preservation of existing vegetation on site shall be demarcated clearly.

6. A concept plan of scale not less than 1 in 1000 indicating the intent of the design with respect to the functions for various parts of the scheme should be included.

3. Irrigation Plan:

The irrigation plan shall be drawn to a scale of not less than 1 in 500 for a site up to one hectare and not less than 1 in 1 000 for site more than one hectare. The Plan shall include the following intonations:

1. The source of irrigation water.
2. Type of water conserving irrigation systems proposed differentiating between systems for different water use zones on the site.
3. Extent of supplementary irrigation provided by water harvesting measures.
4. Arrangement of hydrants or sprinklers indicating location and type with typical details and specifications.

4. Construction Details:

Construction details; specifications and methods used for thc following landscape elements are to be included where applicable:

1. All paved areas for pedestrian and vehicular use, including edges, kerbs, bumper stops, steps, ramps, planters, railings or other protective devices; provision for wheel chair access and movement; Tree protection with tree grating, tree guard, etc.
2. Boundary wall, fence, retaining wall, etc.
3. Structures in landscape such as gatehouses, kiosks, toilets, pergolas, space frame, pools, ponds, water bodies, any other special features, etc.
4. Site utilities such as storm water drains, manholes, catch basins, outdoor lighting fixtures, electric feeder pillars, junction box, fire hydrant, garbage collection points, litter bins, etc.
5. Outdoor signage and street furniture.
6. Play equipment and tot lots where appropriate.
7. Any other relevant detail or information.

D. Protection of Landscape During Construction

Development projects involve disturbance to the existing soil conditions, removal of existing trees and overall change in the microclimate and drainage pattern. Measures to minimize hazardous effects should be put into effect as explained below. Measures for the prevention of soil erosion, sediment control and management of storm water shall be implemented as given below:

1. Timing of Construction:

Construction work and erosion control applications shall be scheduled and sequenced during dry weather periods when the potential for erosion is the lowest. Slope protection techniques to control erosion shall be used when construction during wet season is unavoidable. Sedimentation collection systems, drainage systems, and runoff diversion devices shall be installed before construction activity. The

Landscape Architect/Architect/Engineer-in-charge shall monitor the site conditions and progress of work and schedule appropriate timing and sequencing of construction.

2. Preservation of Existing Vegetation:

Protection of existing vegetation (including trees, shrubs, grasses and other plants) where possible by preventing disturbance or damage to specified areas during construction is recommended. This practice minimizes the amount of bare soil exposed to erosive forces. All existing vegetation shall be marked on a site survey plan. A tree survey in prescribed format shall be carried out. The landscape plan should indicate trees, which have been preserved, and also those, which had to be transplanted or removed clearly differentiating between these three categories.

3. Trees retained on the project site shall be protected during the construction period by following measures:

1. Damage to roots shall be prevented during trenching, placing backfill, driving or parking heavy equipment, dumping of trash, oil, paint, and other materials detrimental to plant health by restricting these activities to outside the area of the canopy of the tree.
2. Trees will not be used for support; their trunks shall not be damaged by cutting and carving or by nailing posters, advertisements or other material.
3. Lighting of fires or carrying out heat or gas emitting construction activity within the ground, covered by canopy of the tree shall not be permitted.
4. Young trees or saplings identified for preservation (height less than 2.00 m, 0.10 m trunk girth at 1.00 m height from finish ground, 2.00 m crown diameter) within the construction site have to be protected using tree guards of approved specification.
5. Existing drainage patterns through or into any preservation area shall not be modified unless specifically directed by the Landscape Architect/Architect/Engineer-in-charge.
6. Existing grades shall be maintained around existing vegetation and lowering or raising the levels around the vegetation is not allowed unless specifically directed by the Landscape Architect/Architect/Engineer-in-charge.
7. Maintenance activities shall be performed as needed to ensure that the vegetation remains healthy.
8. The preserved vegetated area shall be inspected by the Landscape Architect / Architect / Engineer-in-charge at regular intervals so that they remain undisturbed. The date of inspection, type of maintenance or restorative action followed shall be recorded in the logbook.

4. Staging Areas:

Measures shall be followed for collecting runoff from construction areas and material storage sites; diverting water flow away from such polluted areas, so that pollutants do not mix with storm water runoff from undisturbed areas.

Temporary drainage channels, perimeter dike/swale, etc shall be constructed to carry the pollutant-laden water directly to treatment device or facility. The plan shall indicate how the above is accomplished on site, well in advance of the commencing of the construction activity.

5. Preservation of Topsoil:

Topsoil removal and preservation shall be mandatory for development projects larger than 1.00 hectare. Topsoil shall be stripped to a depth of 200 mm from areas proposed to be occupied by buildings, roads, paved areas and external services. Topsoil is rich in organic content and is essential to establish new vegetation. It shall be stockpiled to a height of 400 mm in designated areas and shall be re-applied to site during plantation of the proposed vegetation. Topsoil shall be separated from sub-soil debris and stones larger than 50 mm diameter. The stored topsoil may be used as finished grade for planting areas.

6. Spill Prevention and Control:

Spill prevention and control plans shall be made, clearly stating measures to stop the source of the spill, to contain the spill, to dispose the contaminated material and hazardous wastes, and stating designation of personnel trained to prevent and control spills. Hazardous wastes include pesticides, paints, cleaners, petroleum products, fertilizers and solvents.

7. Measures during Construction:

During construction soil becomes unconsolidated due to removal of stabilizing material such as vegetation and disturbance of stabilized existing grade resulting in loss of topsoil and also deposition in undesirable places. A soil erosion and sedimentation control plan to be prepared prior to construction. The soil erosion, sediment control and storm water practices should be considered while construction is proceeding.

8. Sedimentation Basin:

A temporary dam or basin at the lowest point of the site has to be constructed for collecting, trapping and storing sediment produced by the construction activities, together with a flow detention facility for reducing peak runoff rates. This would allow most of the sediments to settle before the runoff are directed towards the outfall.

9. Contour Trenching:

Contour trenching is an earth embankment or ridge and channel arrangement constructed parallel to the contours along the face of the slope at regular intervals on long and steep slopes (in sloping areas with slopes greater than 10 percent). They are used for reducing runoff velocity and increasing the distance of overland runoff flow, to hold moisture and minimize sediment loading of surface runoff. Vegetative cover of tree and native grasses in the channels may be planted to stabilize the slopes and reduce erosion.

10. Mulching:

Mulching shall be used with seeding and planting in steep slope areas (slopes greater than 33 percent) that are prone to heavy erosion. Netting or anchoring shall be used to hold it in place. Other surface runoff control measures like contour terracing to break up concentrated flows shall be installed prior to seeding and mulching. Materials such as straw, grass, grass hay and compost shall be placed on or incorporated into the soil surface. In addition to stabilizing soils, mulching will reduce the storm water runoff over an area. Together with seeding or planting, mulching aids plant growth by holding the seed, fertilizers and topsoil in place. It retains moisture and insulates the soil against extreme temperatures.

11. Geo-grids

A deformed or non-deformed netlike polymeric material used with foundation, soil, rock, earth or any other geo-technical engineering-related material as an integral part of the human-made project structure or system, caned geo-grids may be used as control measure. On filling with lightly compacted soil or fine aggregate, a monolithic structure is created providing an effective means of confinement for unconsolidated materials within the cells and preventing their movement even on steep slopes. If required the area can then be seeded to maintain, 'green' environment. The junctions have a central opening through which water can permeate ensuring that organic material receives moisture for rapid growth.

E. Soil and Water Conservation

The soil conservation, sediment control and storm water management practices shall be followed after construction is completed.

1. Vegetative Measures:

The vegetative measures shall include the following:

1. Topsoil Laying

This includes the placement of topsoil or other suitable plant material over disturbed lands to provide suitable soil medium for vegetative growth. Topsoil laying shall involve replacing fertile top-soils that were stripped and stock-piled during earlier site development activities; the laid soil shall be stabilized before the next monsoon by planting grass, shrubs and trees.

The following guidelines shall apply to the placement of topsoil:

1. The existing or established grade of sub-soil should be maintained.
2. A *p*H of 6.0 to *7.5* and organic content of not less than *1.5* percent by mass is recommended for topsoil. Where *p*H is less than 6.0, lime shall be applied to adjust *p*H to *6.5* or higher up to *7.5*. Any soils having soluble salt content greater than *500* parts per million shall not be used.
3. Prior to spreading the topsoil, the sub-grade shall be loosened to a depth of *50* mm to permit bonding. Topsoil shall be spread uniformly at a minimum compacted depth of *50* mm on grade of 1:3 or steeper slopes; a minimum depth of 100 mm on shallower slopes is essential. A depth of 300 mm is preferred on relatively flatter land.

2. Planting/Vegetation Cover:

The most effective way to prevent soil erosion, sedimentation and to stabilize disturbed and undisturbed land is through the provision of vegetative cover by effective planting practices. The foliage and roots of plants provide dust control and a reduction in erosion potential by increasing the infiltration, trapping sediment, stabilizing soil, and dissipating the energy of hard rain. Temporary seeding shall be used in areas disturbed after rough grading to provide soil protection until final cover is established. Permanent seeding/planting is used in buffer areas, vegetated swales and steep slopes. The vegetative cover also increases the percolation of rain-water thereby increasing the ground water recharge.

2. Storm Water Management and Filtration Techniques

The surface water flow is increased in urban areas due to predominance of hard surfaces. Storm water management techniques assure conservation of water thereby increasing the ground water recharge. Filters facilitate draining pollutants out from surface water runoff through straining before discharge into the drainage way. Rain-water harvesting and sullage recycle systems need to be implemented on all new constructions over 1000 square meters in urban areas.

3. Rain Water Harvesting Structures in Urban Environment:

1. Water harvesting refers to the collection and storage of rain-water and also harvesting surface and ground water, prevention of loss through evaporation and seepage, and other hydrological and engineering interventions aimed at conserving water.
2. The advantages of using rain water harvesting structures in urban areas are as follows:
   1. Water harvesting recharges ground water and is an ideal solution to water problems in areas with inadequate water resources.
   2. Increase in ground water aquifer level due to methods enhancing infiltration.
   3. Mitigation of the effect of drought.
   4. Reduction of storm water runoff into the public drainage system.
   5. Reduction of flooding of the roads during monsoons.
   6. Removal of pollutants and soil from the storm water runoff.
   7. Reduction of soil erosion.

4. Methods of ground water recharge may be as follows:

1. Recharge pits,
2. Recharge trenches
3. Re-use of abandoned dug wells,
4. Re-use of abandoned hand pumps,
5. Recharge shafts,
6. Lateral shafts with bore wells, and
7. Spreading techniques like percolation ponds, check dams or gabion structures.

5. Structures for Rain-Water Harvesting and Soil and Water Conservation:

1. Infiltration techniques:

1. *Infiltration trenches:* An infiltration trench is a rock filled trench that receives storm water runoff. Storm water passes through a combination of pre-treatment measures, a grass swale and into the trench to be stored in void spaces and then infiltrates into the soil matrix.
2. *Bio-filtration swale/grass swale:* Bio-filtration swales are vegetated channels with a slope similar to that of standard storm drain channels (less than 0.6 percent), but wider and shallower to maximize flow residence time and promote pollutant removal by filtration through the use of properly selected vegetation. It has to be designed to trap particulate pollutants (suspended solids and trace metals), promote infiltration and reduce the flow velocity of the storm water runoff. It shall be integrated with storm water system

3. *Sand filter:* Sand filters are devices that filter storm water runoff through a sand layer into an underground drain system which conveys the water to a detention facility. They are effective in removing total suspended solids. The effectiveness of sand filtration is improved if it is preceded by a grass swale with infiltration trench.

2. Detention facilities:

1. *Wet ponds:* Wet ponds are constructed basins that have a permanent pool of water throughout the year (or at least throughout the wet season). Wet ponds retain the storm water runoff in a permanent pool and facilitate pollution removal through settling and biological update.
2. *Storm water wet lands:* Storm water wet lands are structures similar to wet ponds, which incorporate wetland plants into the design. They have to be designed for treating storm water runoff, and typically have less biodiversity than natural wetland systems. A distinction should be made between using a constructed wet land for storm water management and diverting storm water into natural wetland. The latter is not recommended because it would degrade the resource.
3. *Wet vaults and storage tanks:* Wet vaults and tanks are underground facilities used for the storage of surface water, and typically constructed from reinforced cement concrete (vaults) or corrugated pipes (tanks). The water that is captured in these vaults and tanks may be used later for irrigation.

F. Conservation and Re-use of Water for Irrigation

The following measures shall be followed for design of irrigation systems for landscape works:

1. Water conserving irrigation systems should differentiate between systems for different water use zones on the site. Supplementary irrigation sources should be used by means of appropriate water harvesting measures.
2. The irrigation system should be designed considering the prevailing wind direction, slope and proposed grade, type of soil, soil percolation, and the type of vegetation to be watered.
3. Spray irrigation to be designed to provide total head to head cover to avoid dry spots and spray on to paved areas and unplanted surfaces.
4. Spray irrigation is to be avoided in areas of width less than 3.00 m.
5. Sullage recycle systems are ideal for large housing complexes and residential colonies. Sullage (or water from kitchens and bathrooms) is treated and recycled for gardening and toilet flushing reducing fresh water requirement by 60 percent. Irrigation system should be designed keeping sullage recycle in view.

G. Earth Slopes and Grading Requirements

1. Grading Design:

Design for changes in elevation in the outdoor environment is a primary component of landscape development. Grading of proposed external development areas should relate to the existing topography of the site and it should direct surface water runoff to the designed drainage and water harvesting area. Grading design parameters are as follows:

1. The proposed grading design should respond to the function and purpose of the activities to be accommodated within the site.
2. New development and structures to be integrated with existing landform within the site and in its immediate surroundings.

3. Storm water to be directed away from buildings.
4. Terraces, levels and slopes in required areas to be created and to emphasize control, or negotiate circulation routes and views.
5. Steep slopes to be modified to minimize or eliminate erosion.
6. Legally, grades cannot be changed beyond the property line of the site.
7. The rate of storm water runoff leaving the site after construction to not exceed the preconstruction rate.
8. Grading design should optimize cut and fill.

2. Grading Plan:

1. The submitted grading plan should include the following:

1. All existing features of the site, including all building with plinth level;
2. Structures such as walls, walks, steps, roads, etc;
3. Utilities such as water lines, sewer and storm water drainage, electrical lines, etc; and
4. Utility structures like manholes, junction boxes, sewage treatment plant, septic tank, soak pit, water tanks, water treatment plant, transformers and all underground structures indicated appropriately.

Proposed features shall be indicated in firm lines and existing features in dash.

2. The grading plan should represent:

1. General landform concept graphically represented with appropriate symbols and abbreviations.
2. Proposed contour lines should be integrated with existing and proposed elevations within the project site.
3. Location of swales and surface water flow, surface and sub-surface soil drainage system or water harvesting systems.
4. Location of drainage catchments, areas of retention/detention or disposal/outfall point as the case may be.
5. Spot grades on road, walks, and swales including top level and relevant invert levels of all utilities and utilities structures as mentioned above; critical spot elevation to be established.
6. Spot elevation of building floor finish level, steps, walls, terraces and other such structures.
7. Changes in direction or rate of slope.

3. Spot Elevations

Spot elevations shall be used to supplement contours in the following situations:

1. To indicate variations from the normal slope or gradient between contour lines.
2. To indicate elevations of intersecting planes and lines, like corners of buildings, walls, steps and kerbs.
3. To indicate elevations at top and bottom of vertical elements like walls, steps and kerbs.
4. To indicate floor and entrance elevations.
5. To indicate elevations of high and low points.

6. To indicate top elevations of utilities and utilities structure.

4. Slope Calculation

Slopes are expressed as follows:

1. Percentage (of slope) = Vertical rise × 100/Horizontal distance
   for example = 1 × 100/50 m = 2 percent.
2. Proportion (of slope) = Vertical rise (1.0 m)/Horizontal distance
   for example = I in 50 m or 1:50
3. Degree of slope, expressed as angle
   for example 10°, 15°, etc.
5. Typical Grading Symbols and Abbreviations

Table 11.1.

	Symbol	*Description*
1	– – (100) – –	Existing contour
2	– 100 –	Proposed contour
3	(100.5)	Existing spot elevation
4	100.5 (Bold)	Proposed spot elevation
5	CB	Catch basin
6.	FFL	Finished floor level
7	FGL	Finished ground level
8	TW/BW	Top of wall/Bottom of wall
9	TK/BK	Top of kerb/Bottom of kerb
10	HP/LP	High point/Low point
11	IL	Invert level

H. PLANTING DESIGN CONSIDERATIONS

Plant materials are a very important component of landscape design, and planting design is integral to the landscape plan. Designing with plants requires awareness and knowledge of a broad range of aspects including (*a*) ecology, (*b*) botany, (*c*) horticulture, (*d*) aesthetic value, (*e*) growth and survival, and (*f*) use of plants to fulfill environmental design functions.

1. Plant Material:

The major sets of factors that influence the choice of plant material are related to the characteristics, both botanical and physical of plant material and the context in which the plant material is to be used. The interrelationship of these sets of factors is the basis for developing a sound approach to the process of designing with plants.

2. Physical and Botanical Characteristics of Plant Material:

The information on plant material should be available in a systematic format to include definition, significance and design implications of the following aspects:

1. Nomenclature (botanical and trade-name);
2. Origin, family and natural habitat;
3. Growth characteristic and form as a function of habit;
4. Physical characteristics, for example bark texture, foliage, etc;
5. Propagation and maintenance; and
6. Use in landscape design.

3. Vegetation Types (Evergreen and Deciduous):

Some examples of the functional implications of using evergreen and deciduous plant material for specific situations are:

1. Evergreen trees for:

1. Places requiring shade throughout the year,
2. Strong visual screening,
3. Part of windbreak or shelter planting, and
4. Areas where leaf litter is to be discouraged.

2. Deciduous trees for:

1. Greater visual variety,
2. Partial visual barrier,
3. Areas where under-planting is to be encouraged (for example grass),
4. Emphasis on branching and flowering pattern, and
5. Areas where shade is not required throughout the year.

4. Growth Rate and Age of the Vegetation:

Growth rate is directly related to the life-span of a tree and slower growing trees have a life-span extending to hundreds of years. The fast growing trees to the exclusion of slower growing varieties is not recommended. Landscapes are developed to sustain future generations; slow growing long lived native trees shall be emphatically included in all major planting schemes, especially those related to institutional campuses and large urban development. However, fast growing species do have a limited role, and are appropriate in situations where:

1. Quick effects are required, for example in wind-breaks and shelterbelts.
2. Immediate results with regards to stabilization of soil, etc are necessary, as for example, in soil conservation schemes.
3. As 'nurse plants' to protect slower growing sensitive species when necessary.

The slower growing species would generally be appropriate in situations where sustained environmental benefits are required such as roadside planting, campuses, townships, industrial areas, and other public landscapes.

5. Growth Habits of Various Kinds of Vegetation and their Form:

The overall physical form of a plant is usually the result of the foliage density and branching pattern. It may also be expressed as the proportionate relations between height and canopy spread. The latter is direct expression of growth habit.

A number of classifications of tree by their overall form exist, but it is almost impossible to have a variety according to regional conditions. The following classification into basic types may be useful:

1. *Trees of fastigiated or columnar habit:* Examples of trees of this type are:

- Casurina equisitifolia (Beet-wood)
- Grevillea robusta (Silver oak)
- Polyathia longifolia (Ashok)
- Populus species (Poplar).

Though the branching pattern of each is different, the overall shape is similar.

2. *Tall trees with broad canopy:* Examples of trees of this type are:

- Dalbergia sissoo (Sheesham)
- Tamarindus indica (Imli)
- Tenninalia arjuna (Arjun).

The canopy shape does not fit into any specific geometrical category.

3. *Trees of spreading habit:* Examples of trees of this type are:

- Delonix regia (Gulmohar)
- Lagerstromiaflosreginae (Pride of India)
- Pithecolobium saman (Rain Tree).

Though these trees vary greatly in size, their basic form is similar.

4. *Trees of weeping habit:* Examples of trees of this type are:
   - Callistemon lanceolatus (Bottle brush)
   - Salix babylonica (Weeping willow).

The above classification is helpful in choosing various combinations of the above types to achieve desired function and visual objectives.

6. Foliage Characteristics of Plant Material:

Visual effects imparted by vegetation, for example, the perceived visual textures of plant forms depend on:

1. *Leaf size and shape*: Examples of plants with large leaves and bold foliage texture are:
   - *Alstonia scholaris* (Chattin Saptporni)
   - *Delonix regia* (Gulmohar)
   - *Jacaranda miosaefolia* (Nili Gulmohar)
   - *Plumeria acutifolia* (Temple Tree)
   - *Pterospermum acerifolium* (Kanak Champa).

   Leaf shape can also determine the appearance of the foliage of the plant, as for example:
   - *Acacia auriculaeformis* (Australian Black wood): Long narrow leaves
   - *Callistemon lanceolatus* (Bottle Brush): Narrow leaves giving a feathery appearance
   - *Polyalthia longifolia* (Ashok): Long narrow leaves
   - *Salix babylonica* (Weeping willow): Narrow leaves giving a feathery appearance.
2. *Leaf texture*: The textural appearance of a plant is the result of the play of light and shade on the foliage. Plants with larger leaves generally appear bolder in texture than smaller leaves plants as the areas of light and shade are larger and therefore more clearly differentiated.
3. *Leaf and foliage colour*: Most trees in India have foliage in varying shades of green with variations in colour at the time of leaf fall and at the period when the tree is newly in leaf, when the leaves are fresh and much lighter in colour. Examples are:
   - *Lagerstroemia speciosa* (Jarul) - Leaves acquire reddish tinge before falling
   - *Polyalthia longifolia* (Ashok), *Delonix regia* (Gulmohar), *Erythrina indica* (India coral tree), etc: Leaves turn yellow before falling
   - *Ficus, intectoria (Pilkhan) Mangifera indica* (Mango) etc: Young leaves have reddish tinge.
4. *Foliage density and distribution*: An important consideration is the way in which particular kinds of vegetation are perceived. Tree masses are usually seen from greater distance than shrub areas; foliage texture of different distinctive kinds of trees growing together has to be markedly distinctive for individual species to be recognizably apparent. In shrub areas subtle differences in foliage texture may suffice for creating the required visual effect.

7. Flowering Characteristics of Plant Material:

Important considerations while classifying plant material according to flowering characteristics are as follows:

1. Season,
2. Density and distribution of flowers on the plant,
3. Botanical characteristics of flowers (for example single/cluster, etc),
4. Colour, and
5. Presence or absence of foliage during flowering period.

8. For the purpose of understanding the visual effect of flowers, tree species may be divided into two types:

1. Trees on which flowers appear in profusion and therefore have a very strong visual impact, for example Delonu regia, Cassia fistula, Lagerstroemiaflosreginae.
2. Those on which flowers are less profuse, or perhaps last for a shorter period and visual impact is more subtle, for example Thespesia spp., Bauhinia spp., etc.

An additional consideration when choosing shrubs for their flowering quality is the visual appearance of the flowers themselves, as shrubs are usually seen from quite close. Distinctive flowers are those of

1. *Beleperone guttata* (Shrimp plant),
2. *Hibiscus rosa-sinensis* (Clinex hibiscus),
3. *Iasminum sambac* (Chameli),
4. *Tabemaemontana coronaria* (Cape jasmine), and
5. *Thevetia peruviana* (Yellow oleander).

9. The characteristics like odour of flowers may be an added benefit of flowering plants. Flowers with distinctive scent include those of Harsingar *(Nyctanthes arbor-tristis),* Chameli *(Jasminum pubescens),* Raat Ki Rani *(Cestrum noctumum),* etc.

10. Flowering characteristics of plant material may be classified as per the following format:

Table 11.2

Botanical name	Characteristics of flower	Seasonal duration	Visual impact

11. Growth Requirement of Plant Material:

Information about growth requirements of plant material applicable in landscape design pertains to the ability of particular plants to survive in specific environmental situations. These environmental conditions may arise from a number of aspects. Capacity of plants to grow in cultivated situations is related to the environmental conditions in their natural habitat.

12. Soil conditions:

Physical as well as chemical properties of the available soil are important. These may or may not be amenable to change; they would therefore affect the choice of plant material considerably. Physical properties include consideration of light (for example sandy) and heavy (for example clayey) soils, and their structure.

Chemical properties pertain to the presence or absence of nutrients and salts; soil, alkalinity or acidity. A preliminary soil analysis is essential for implementing effective planting schemes.

13. Availability and quality of water:

The water requirement may be derived by data of humidity and rainfall of plants natural habitat. The water table of the area where the plantation is to be done has a crucial bearing on the design with plants as well as a financial implication for reduced maintenance if planted appropriately.

14. Availability of sunlight:

The growth rate of plants are directly related to sunlight availability; such as plants that require (a) full sunlight, (b) partial sunlight, (c) predominantly shade, and (d) complete shade.

15. Quality of air:

Growth may be affected by chemical pollutants such as sulphur dioxide or physical pollution such as dust. Certain plants have the ability to withstand pollution, such plants are imperative for industrial areas, roads, highways, etc.

16. Maintenance:

The success of a designed landscape depends upon the growth of vegetation over an extended period of time; therefore maintenance of landscape is also a design component. Maintenance needs and practices in any given situation arise out of the inter-relationship between the growth requirements of plant material chosen and the environmental conditions existing on site.

The likely degree of maintenance should be assessed based on the following:

1. Scale of the design project,
2. Financial and manpower resource,
3. Availability of manures,
4. Future intensity of site, and
5. Environmental conditions.

In small scale projects such as gardens and small parks, the natural environmental conditions can be changed and maintained by management practices such as irrigation and application of fertilisers. The choice of plant species is therefore not very strictly limited by the existing environmental conditions. On larger scale schemes, such as very large parks, campuses and townships, this kind of intensive maintenance may not be possible. The process of choosing plants shall therefore respond to the existing environmental conditions and also in such cases the choice of plant material is restricted by these conditions and suitable species become limited. The type of treatment adopted, as given below, may also serves as a guide to the degree of maintenance required:

Table 11.3

1.	**Low Maintenance**	The lowest degree of maintenance is usually possible in areas treated with native species of trees only. A slightly higher degree is necessary where native shrubs are also used, as these may require pruning.
2.	**Medium**	Areas treated with a mixture of native and exotic trees. Exotic shrubs and trees.
3.	**High**	Exotic shrubs and ground covers. Lawns and maintained grass areas. Annual flowers and special schemes.

17. Functional Aspects of Design with Plants:

Plant materials in landscape design may be used to

1. Improve existing environmental conditions with respect to soil, drainage, microclimate, air pollution;
2. Create a designed physical environment through the organization of open space; and
3. Interpret and express the contemporary understanding of the man-nature relationship, that is, design with plants on an ecological rather than horticultural basis.

18. Choosing of Plant Material:

Two sets of factors influence the choice of plant material in landscape design. One relates to information about plant material itself, which determines the suitability of plant material from the point of view of growth requirements of plant material, and physical characteristics of the plant material. The second relates to the situation for which a planting proposal has to be made that pertains to the context in which the plant materials have to be used. Considerations of scale (that is, regional, local or very small scale situations), the existing environmental conditions, and functions which the plant material has to fulfill are important. Also the level of maintenance which is likely to be kept up has to be considered which is especially important on very large sites. The biological history and ecological need of exotic plant should be studied prior to introduction in the landscape schemes to avoid the hazard of the species that may become invasive.

The factors determining choice of plant materials may be thus summarized as follows:

1. *Environmental conditions existing on site*: These include climatic, soil characteristics, water table, etc.
2. *Functions which plant material has to fulfill in specific situations on a given site*: These may be either environmental functions (pertaining to improvement of soil conditions, modification or microclimate, etc) or design functions relating to creating spaces enclosure, framing views, providing visual relief, etc.
3. *Physical characteristics and growth requirements of plant material*: The former include foliage density, foliage texture, leaf size and shape, flower colour, rooting characteristics, etc., The latter include moisture requirements, whether the plant grows in sunny or shaded conditions, etc.

18. Methodology of Design with Plants:

The process for designing with plants on a given site condition may be as per the format given below:

Table 11.4

Zone	Characteristics	Functions	Form	Species chosen	Remarks

Plant material used in landscape design may be broadly classified as:

Table 11.5

1.	**Tree**	Large, Medium, Small
2.	**Shrub**	Tall, Low
3.	**Ground cover**	Very low shrubs less than a 300 mm high

19. Functions of Plant Material:

1. Trees:

Trees perform the following functions:

1. Protecting soil,
2. Modifying microclimate,
3. Shade,
4. Habitat,
5. Enclosure,
6. Direction and framing views,
7. Screening,
8. Visual relief, and
9. Ornamental.

2. Shrubs:

The functions are similar to those of trees. Shrubs may be used together with trees to reinforce the functions, for example, noise barrier, shelter belts, enclosures, etc. Other forms in which shrubs may be used are:

1. *Hedges*: These require regular maintenance
2. *Shrubbery*: Here plants are allowed to retain their natural shape; they therefore require little maintenance.

Shrubs provide barriers, which may either be visual or physical (hedges). Barriers may be required in a range of situations, for example they may be only for defining space, or they may be required to be impenetrable for security.

3. Ground cover:

Ground cover plants are those which naturally grow to a very low height. Some of the uses for which they may be used are:

1. Stabilizing soil on steep slopes such as embankments.
2. As a low maintenance substitute for grass (where the surface is not to be used).
3. For providing variety in surface treatment.
4. Contrast with paving materials, for example to soften rigid lines of paving.
5. As a subtle means of demarcating space, as for example, in places where tall plants would be visually intrusive.
6. In combination with other plants to provide contrast or harmony in form.

4. Climbers:

Certain climbers because of their spreading habits may also be used as ground cover (for example *Asparagus* spp.) Climbers are useful for shading exposed walls from direct sunlight. They may also be used for stabilizing soil on embankments (for example, *Ficus stipulata, Ipomea biloba).* On sites where a high degree of security makes fencing necessary, climbers and spreading plants like Bougainvillea species may be trained on boundary wall.

5. Planting for Shelter and Soil Conservation:

The use of vegetation for controlling wind is widely recognized as an effective way of conserving soil and reducing erosion by wind. Vegetation may therefore be used for modifying the microclimate, by obstructing, guiding, deflecting or filtering wind current. Vegetation areas designed to fulfill these general functions are usually classified as windbreakers and shelterbelts. Wind-breaker is grown to protect planting around gardens and orchards. Windbreakers generally consist of single or double row of trees. Shelterbelt provides an extensive barrier of trees with several rows of trees. Plant species are chosen with particular regard to their physical and growth characteristics, and their effectiveness in achieving the desired results. Both wind-breakers and shelterbelts have considerable visual impact in the landscape in which they are situated. They therefore need to be designed, so that they make a positive visual and aesthetic contribution to their environment.

6. Function:

Windbreakers and shelterbelts fulfill essential micro-climatic functions in rural and urban environments. Benefits accruing from plantation of shelter planting may be as follows:

1. Reduction in wind velocity resulting in the arrest of movements of sand and soil particles.
2. Prevention of soil erosion.
3. Modification of micro-climate; moderation of change in air temperature.
4. Protection of crops from being blown by high winds.

5. Protection of livestock.
6. Reduction in evaporation of soil moisture. Increase in soil moisture content varies from 3 percent to 7.8 percent. Water loss due to evaporation is lessened.
7. Increase in soil moisture due to greater dew fall in sheltered areas has been found to be 200 percent higher than on exposed ground; heaviest dew fall is over a distance of 2 to 3 times the height of the shelterbelt.
8. Beneficial effect on growth of plants that are affected by high winds.
9. Extensive shelterbelts may also be used to augment the supply of fuel in rural areas.
10. The zone of influence of shelterbelt on crop yield extends to a distance of 20 times the height of the belt, with the maximum effect being observed 10 times the height of the tree belt, on the leeward side.

7. Wind Erosion:

Some of the basic functions of windbreaks and shelterbelts in arid and semi-arid areas are to conserve soil and reduce erosion by wind. The latter is a natural phenomenon in and lands having very little rainfall (125 mm-250 mm) and in areas adjoining a river, lake or sea. Wind erosion is a serious problem in areas where the ground is virtually bare and devoid of vegetation.

Factors which influence the degree and kind of wind erosion are as follows:

1. Features of wind: Speed, direction, temperature, humility, burden carried, etc.
2. Character of surface: Rough or smooth plant cover, obstruction, temperature, etc.
3. Topography: Flat, undulating, broken, etc.
4. Character of soil: Texture, organic matter, moisture content, etc.

8. Techniques for control of wind erosion:

The principal method of reducing surface velocity of wind, upon which depends the abrasive and transportation capacity of wind, is by vegetation measures. Vegetation methods are found to be most effective in the form of windbreaks and shelterbelts.

In aerodynamic terms, these provide protection as follows:

1. Sheltered zone on the leeward side extends to approximately 15-30 times the height of the belt.
2. A dense belt provides greater shelter immediately to, leeward side but the sheltered area is not as extensive as when a more permeable zone of vegetation is provided.
3. Porosity is important in the effectiveness of shelterbelt and proper selection of tree species is necessary. Porosity near ground level is desirable.
4. Effectiveness of shelter planting depends more on height and permeability than on width. The width influences the general microclimate but above a certain minimum width, it does not effect greater reduction in wind velocity.

Protection obtained varies in relation to height (H) of shelterbelts, as given below:

Table 11.6.

	Distance	Wind Reduced by (in percent)
1.	H	90
2.	2H	75
3.	5H	50
4.	1OH	20

This indicates that it is better to have several windbreaks 5H to 6H apart rather than large forest stands with wide open spaces in between.

9. Profiles:

A belt which rises and falls abruptly on windward and leeward sides is said to be more effective. Smaller trees and shrubs should occupy the inter-spaces between the tall trees. The depth of the shelterbelt should be approximately ten times its height. This is, however, only a thumb rule. Much lesser widths of 20 m to 30 m have also been found to be useful in particular situations; 15 m should be considered as minimum width. Apart from factors such as climate, soil, fast rate of growth, one of the more significant considerations in choosing species for shelter planting is the possibility of a particular species serving the dual role of wood-production (for fuel, fodder) as well as shelter.

10. Spacing of plants in windbreaks and shelterbelts:

Windbreaks usually consist of a single or double row of trees planted at 0.7 m to 1.5 m according to species. Normally, one year old trees are used. As the roots of tree extend for some distance beyond the rows in which they are planted, the same should be taken into account while planting windbreakers. The most common layout where shelter planting is part of an extensive planned programme, is that of tree belts arranged in a chessboard pattern, each field being-protected from every side. This pattern gives full protection to all the fields, provided that the right distance between the fields has been chosen. Efficient protection is achieved if belts are separated by a distance of not more than 20 times the height of the trees. A considerable mixture of species is recommended so as to compensate for different rates of growth and also to achieve variety in the form of crowns.

Within shelterbelts, close spacing of tree is the general practice. The recommended spacing for shrubs is I.0m and for tree such as Casuarina and Grevellia robusta (Silver Oak) 2.5m. Spacing between rows should be 2.3 m to 3 m to enable mechanized cultivation. Five rows of tree and shrubs are considered necessary for protection.

11. Management:

Shelterbelts should be regarded as living groups of trees to be managed in perpetuity and the following shall be taken into consideration for management thereof:

1. Thinning are limited to a strict minimum.

2. Cutting is done individually by single tree selection method.
3. Continuous cultivation may be required in areas with scanty rainfall.
4. If individual trees do not survive, they should be replaced immediately to avoid gaps in the vegetation belt.

The shelterbelt should be protected from cattle, either by fencing or other means, specially in the early stages. The location of shelterbelt may be related to local features such as public and private road networks, buildings, irrigation and water conservation works and methods of soil management practice (contour bunding, contour cultivation etc). Careful choice of site will provide maximum protection to adjacent land and give shelter and shade.

The application of the concept of shelterbelts to landscape planning and design may be effective in the creation of landscape structure of very large developments at the regional scale, or townships or campuses. Shelterbelts can also be established in association with, or instead of road side planting. This creates a distinctive landscape pattern. The advantage of using native species in shelter planting is:

1. New development is merged into the existing landscape keeping the original character of the landscape.
2. The shelterbelt is a component of land management (previous waste or barren land is conserved).
3. Additional habitat for wildlife is brought into existence.

12. Species-suitable for wind breaks are:

1. For Dry and Arid Regions :

- Acacia auriculiformis (Australian Blackwood)
- Ailanthus excelsa (Maharukh)
- Albilzia lebbeck (Siris)
- Azadiracta indica (Neem)
- Casuarina equisetifolia (Beef-wood)
- Dalbergia sissoo (Sisham)
- Eugeniajambolana (Jamun)
- Grevillea robusta (Silver oak)
- Peltophorumferrugineum (Cooper pod)
- Tamarindus indica (Imli)
- Pongamia glabra (Indian beech)
- Tamarix articulata (Tamarisk)

2. For Coastal Area :

- Anacardium occidentale (Cashu)
- Ailanthus malabarica (Alston)

- Cassuarina equisetifolia (Beef-wood)
- Pongamia glabra (Indian beech)
- Sesbania aculeate (Sesban)
- Thevetia peruvian (Yellow oleander)
- Thespesia populnea (Indian Tulip)
- Vitex negundo (Sephali)

13. Air Pollution Control by Plants:

Air pollution may be caused by areas or point sources such as cities, industrial areas, factories or by linear sources such as highways. Vegetation buffers can minimize the build-up of pollution levels in urban areas, by acting as pollution sinks.

Studies have established that air pollution, smoke and sulphur dioxide leads to aggravation of chronic respiratory diseases and they are linked to lung cancer, pneumonia, tuberculosis, chest disease in children, stomach cancer and cardiovascular diseases. Lead from vehicle exhausts may have an adverse effect on mental health of children; asbestos from disintegrating clutch and brake linings has been considered as a causal factor in lung cancer.

14. Effect of Plants:

Plant leaves function as efficient gas exchange systems. Their internal structure allows rapid diffusion of water-soluble gases. These characteristics allow the plant to respire and photosynthesis, and they can also remove pollutant from the air. Some of the beneficial results of plantations may be:

1. They are good absorbers of sulphur dioxide.
2. Parks with trees have an SO_2 level lower than city streets.
3. Roadside hedges can reduce traffic generated air borne lead, on leeward side.
4. Heavy roadside planting in the form of shelterbelts can result in a reduction in airborne lead.
5. Complete dust interception can be achieved by a 30 m belt of trees. Even a single row of trees may bring about 25 percent reduction in airborne particulate.

15. Choosing Plants:

The three main criteria for selection of plants may be:

1. Tree, shrubs should have dense foliage with a large surface area, because leaves absorb pollutants.
2. Evergreen trees are found to be more effective.
3. The species chosen must be resistant to pollutants, particularly in the early stages of their growth.

The following species may be examined for their likely potential for pollution control:

- Acacia arabica (Babul)

- Citrus species
- Dyospyros species
- Ficus bengalensis (Banyan)
- Ficus religiosa (Peepal)
- Lilium spp. (Lily)
- Polyalthia lotigifolia (Ashok)
- Tamarindus indica (lmli)
- Thuja occidentalis (Cedar)
- Prosopis luliflora (Mesquite)
- Zizypus jujuba (Jujuba), etc.

Filtering of pollutants is most effective when plants are close to the source of pollution. The design of shelterbelts against pollution is similar to those for protection from wind. They should be permeable to encourage air turbulence and mixing within the belt; there should be no large gaps. The profile should be rough and irregular and should present a tall vertical leading edge to the wing. Spaces should be left within the shelterbelt to allow gravity settlement of particles.

16. Applications:

Air pollution shelterbelts may be used to protect sensitive land uses from air pollution. For instance school playgrounds, children play area and residential estates close to major roads may be so protected. Shelterbelt protection may also be provided for hospitals, institutions, etc, where the vegetation may also be a visual screen and a partial noise barrier. Vegetation may also be used where the existing means of pollution control have proved inadequate.

I. Specifications for Planting Works

The requirements relating to plant materials and other materials; execution of work of tree planting, shrub planting and grassing; maintenance; etc shall be as given below. The contractor shall furnish all materials, labour and related items necessary to complete the work indicated on drawing and specified herein and shall carry out maintenance of the premises for 12 months after completion of the work or as specified by the landscape architect.

1. Plant Materials:

Plant materials shall be well formed and shaped true to type, and free from disease, insects and defects such as knots, windburn, injuries, abrasion or disfigurement. All plant materials shall be healthy, sound, and vigorous, free from disease, insect pests, or their eggs, and shall have healthy, well-developed root systems. All plants shall be hardy under climatic conditions similar to those in the locality of the project. Plants supplied shall conform to the names listed on both the plan and the plant list. No plant material will be accepted if branches are damaged or broken. All material shall be protected from sun and adverse weather until planted. Nursery stock shall be inspected and approved by the landscape architect and the horticulturist/botanist shall do the botanical authenticity of the selected species. All plants shall conform to the requirements specified in the plant list, except those plants larger than specified may be used if approved, but use of such plants shall not increase the contract price. If the use of the larger plant is approved, the spread of roots or ball of earth shall be increased in proportion to the size of the plant. Plants shall be delivered with legible identification labels. The minimum acceptable size of all trees after pruning with branches in normal positions, will conform to the measurement specified in the bill of quantities unless stated otherwise. Caliper measurement will be taken at a point on the trunk 1.0 m above natural ground. All trees supplied shall have terminal shoots. All specimen trees shall have a minimum crown spread of not less than half the size of the overall height.

2. Topsoil (Good Earth) with *p*H Range between 6.5 to 7.5:

Topsoil or good earth shall be a friable loam; typical of cultivated top soils of the locality contains at least 2 percent of decayed organic matter (humus). It shall be taken from a well-drained arable site. It shall be free of sub-soil, stones, earth clods, sticks, roots or other objectionable extraneous matter or debris. It shall contain no toxic material. No topsoil shall be delivered in a muddy condition.

3. Fertilizer:

Dry farm yard manure shall be used. Measurement shall be in stacks, with 8 percent reduction for payment. It shall be free from extraneous matter, harmful bacteria insects or chemicals.

4. Root System:

The root system shall be conducive to successful transplantation. Where necessary, the root-ball shall be preserved by support with hessian or other suitable material. On soils where retention of a good ball is not possible, the roots should be suitably protected in some other way which should not cause any damage to roots .

5. Condition:

Trees and shrubs shall be substantially free from pests and diseases, and shall be materially undamaged. Torn or lacerated roots shall be pruned before dispatch. No roots shall be subjected to adverse conditions, such as prolonged exposure to adverse conditions, such as prolonged exposure to drying winds or subjection to water logging, between lifting and delivery.

6. Marking:

Each specimen of tree and shrub, or each bundle, shall be legibly labeled with the following:

1. Its name.
2. Name of the supplier, unless otherwise agreed.
3. Date of dispatch from the nursery.

7. Fine Grading:

Grades will be smooth and even on a uniform plane without abrupt changes or pockets and slope away from the buildings. The nominated landscape contractor will verify the surface drainage of planting areas and notify the landscape architect of any discrepancies, obstructions or other conditions considered detrimental to proper execution of the work and plant growth.

8. Landscape:

Landscape, work will be tied to the existing condition such as existing trees palms, landscape features, utility lines, pavement kerbs.

etc. Finished grade will bear proper relationship to such control. The nominated landscape contractor shall adjust all works as necessary to meet the conditions and fulfill the intention of the drawings.

After initial settlement the finish grade will be:

1. Turf: 20 mm lower than adjacent walks/kerbs.
2. Shrubs and Ground covers: 40 mm lower than adjacent walks/kerbs.

Prior to planting operation, the contractor will ensure all planting areas free of weeds, debris, rocks over 25 mm in diameter and clumps of earth that do not break up.

9. Trees should be supplied with adequate protection as approved. After delivery, if planting is not to be carried out immediately, balled plants should be placed cheek to cheek and the ball covered with sand to prevent drying out. Bare rooted plants can be heeled in by placing the roots in a prepared trench and covering them with earth which should be watered in to avoid air pockets round the roots.

10. Digging of Pits:

Tree pits shall be dug a minimum of three weeks prior to backfilling. The pits shall be 1200 mm in diameters and 1: 200 mm deep. While digging the pits, the topsoil up to a depth of 300 mm may be kept aside, if found good (depending upon site conditions), and mixed with the rest of the soil. If the soil is bad below, it shall be replaced with the soil mixture as specified further herein. If the soil is normal it shall be mixed with manure; river sand shall be added to the soil if it is heavy.

11. Flooding of Pits to Reduce Air Pockets:

The soil backfilled, watered through and gently pressed down, a day previous to planting, to make sure that it may not further settle down after planting. The soil shall be pressed down firmly by treading it down, leaving a shallow depression all round for watering.

12. Planting:

No tree pits shall be dug until final tree positions have been pegged out for approval. Care shall be taken that the plant sapling when planted is not buried deeper than in the nursery, or in the pot. Planting should not be carried out in waterlogged soil. Trees should be planted up to the original soil depth; the soil marks on the stem is an indication of this and it should be maintained on the finished level, allowing for setting of the soil after planting. All plastic and other imperishable containers should be removed before planting. Any broken or damaged roots should be cut back to sound growth.

The bottom of the planting pit should be covered with 50 mm to 75 mm of soil. Bare roots should be spread evenly in the planting pit; and small mound in the centre of the pits on which the roots are placed will aid an even spread. Soil should be placed around the roots, gently shaking the trees to allow soil particles to shift into the root system to ensure close contact with all roots and to prevent air pockets. Back fill soil should be firm as filling proceeds, layer by layer, care being taken to avoid damaging the roots.

13. Staking:

Newly planted trees shall be held firmly although not rigidly by staking to prevent a pocket forming around the stem and newly formed fibrous roots being broken by mechanical pulling as the tree rocks.

The main methods of staking shall be:

1. A single vertical stake, 900 mm longer than the clear stem of the tree, driven 600 mm to 900 mm into the soil.
2. Two stakes as above driven firmly on either side of the tree with cross-bar to which the stem is attached (suitable for small bare-rooted or balled material).
3. A single stake driven in at an angle 45° and leaning towards the prevailing wind, the stem just below the lowest branch being attached to the stake (suitable for small bare-rooted or balled material). The end of stake should be pointed and the lower 1 m to 1.2m should be coated with non-injurious wood preservative allowing at least 150 mm above ground level.

14. Tying:

Each tree should be firmly secured to the stake so as to prevent excessive movement. Abrasion shall be avoided by using a buffer, rubber or hessian, between the tree and stake. The tree should be secured at a point just below its lowest branch, and also just above ground level; normally two ties should be used for tree. These should be adjusted or replaced to allow for growth.

15. Watering:

The contractor should allow for the adequate watering in all newly planted trees and shrubs immediately after planting and shall, during the following growing season, keep the plant material well watered.

16. Shrub Planting in Planters and Beds:

1. All areas to be planted with shrubs shall be excavated, trenched to a depth of 750 mm, refilling the excavated earth after breaking clods and mixing with manure in the ratio 8: 1 (8 parts of stacked volume of earth after reduction by 20 percent; 1 part of stacked volume of manure after reduction by 8 percent).
2. Tall shrubs may need staking: which shall be provided if approved by the landscape architect depending upon the conditions of individual plant specimen.
3. For planting shrubs and ground cover shrubs in planters, good earth shall be mixed with manure in proportion as above and filled in planters.
4. Positions of shrubs to be planted should be marked out in accordance with the planting plan. When shrubs are set out, precautions should be taken to prevent root drying. Planting holes 400 mm in diameter and 400 mm deep should be excavated for longer shrubs. Polythene and other non-perishable containers should be removed and any badly damaged roots carefully pruned. The shrubs should then be set in holes so that the soil level, after settlement, will be at the original soil mark on the stem of the shrub. The hole should be back-filled to half its depth and firmed by treading. The remainder of the soil may then be returned and again firmed by treading.

17. Grassing:

1. Preparation:

During the period prior to planting the ground shall be maintained free from weeds. Grading and final leveling of the lawn shall be completed at least three weeks prior to the actual sowing. Regular watering shall be continued until sowing by dividing the lawn area into portions of approximately 5 square meters by constructing small bunds to retain water. These bunds shall be leveled just prior to sowing of grass plants. At the time of actual planting of grass, it shall be ensured that the soil has completely settled.

2. Soil:

The soil itself shall be ensured to the satisfaction of the landscape architect to be a good fibrous loam, rich in humus.

3. Sowing the Grass Roots:

Grass roots shall be obtained from a grass patch, seen and approved beforehand. The grass roots stock received at site shall be manually cleared of all weeds and water sprayed over the same after keeping the stock in a place protected from sun and dry winds. Grass stock received at site may be stored for a maximum of three days. In case grassing for some areas is scheduled for a later date fresh stock of grass roots shall be ordered and obtained. Small roots shall be planted about 75 mm apart into the prepared grounds. Grass areas will only be accepted as reaching practical completion when germination has proved satisfactory and all weeds have been removed.

4. Maintenance:

As soon as the grass is approximately 30 mm high it shall be rolled with a light wooden roller in fine, dry weather - and when it has grown to 50 mm to 80 mm above ground, weeds shall be removed and regular cutting with the scythe and rolling shall be begun. A top-dressing of farm yard manure, bone meal at the rate of 50 g/m^2 and NPK at the rate of 10 g/m^2 shall be applied when the grass is sufficiently secure in the ground to bear the mowing machine, the blades shall be raised 25 mm above the normal level for the first two or three cuttings. That is to say, the grass should be cut so that it is from 40 mm to 50 mm in length, instead of the 30 mm necessary for mature grass. In the absence of rain, in the monsoon the lawn shall be watered with sprinklers every, three days soaking the soil to a depth of at least 200 mm. Damage, failure or dying back of grass due to neglect of watering specially for seeding out of normal season shall be the responsibility of the contractor.

Any shrinkage below the specified levels during the contract or defects liability period shall be rectified at the contractor's expense. The contractor shall exercise care in the use of rotary cultivator and mowing machines to reduce to a minimum the hazards of flying stones and brickbats. All rotary mowing machines are to be fitted with safety guards.

5. Rolling:

Lawn mower with roller shall be used periodically, taking care that the lawn is not too wet and sodden.

6. Edgings:

These shall be kept neat and shall be cut regularly with the edging shears.

7. Watering:

Water shall be applied at least once in three days during dry weather. Water whenever done should be thorough and should wet the soil at least up to a depth of 200 mm.

8. Weeding:

Prior to regular mowing the contractor shall carefully remove rank and unsightly weeds.

9. Maintenance:

1. The landscape contractor shall maintain all planted areas within the landscape contract boundaries for one year until the area is handed over in whole or in phases. Maintenance shall include replacement of dead plants, watering, weeding, cultivating, control of insects, fungus and other diseases by means of spraying with an approved insecticide or fungicide, pruning, and other horticulture operations necessary for the proper growth of the plants and for keeping the landscape contract area neat in appearance.

2. Pruning and Repairs:

Upon completion of planting work under the contract all trees should be pruned and all injuries repaired where necessary. The amount of pruning shall be limited to the minimum necessary to remove dead or injured twigs and branches and to compensate for the loss of roots and result of transplanting operations. Pruning and removal of any part of plant materials should be done with clean sharp tools. Tools used to carry out the pruning work shall be appropriate for the task. The surface of tools and equipment will be sterilized after use on the plant materials that are suspected or known to be diseased. Cuts on plant materials shall be made into the living tissues to induce hardening. Cut surface will be flat, sharp and without jagged or torn edges.

Pruning shall be done in such a manner as not to change the natural habitat or special shape of the trees. Pruning operation will consider carefully the natural growth pattern of branches on the tree, palm or shrub. Tree branches will be pruned back to the collar at the base of the branch.

3. Tree guards:

Where tree guards are necessary, care should be taken to ensure that they do not impede natural movement or restrict growth.

4. Nursery Stock:

Planting should be carried out as soon as possible after reaching the site. Where planting needs to be delayed, care should be taken to protect the plants from pilfering or damage from people or animals. Plants with bare roots should be heeled-in as soon as received or otherwise protected from drying out, and others set closely together and protected from the wind. If planting needs to be delayed for more than a week, packed plants should be unpacked, the bundles opened up and each group of plants heeled-in separately and clearly labeled. If for any reason the surface of the roots becomes dry the roots should be thoroughly soaked before planting.

5. Protective Fencing:

According to local environment shrubs shall be protected adequately from vandalism until established.

6. Routine Maintenance Work Schedule:

Table 11.7

S. No.	Operation	Frequency
1.	Watering	Checking all planting areas and pits and water as often as necessary to ensure that planting material does not dry out
2.	Weeding	Monthly

S. No.	Operation	Frequency
3.	Edging	Monthly
4.	Fertilizing	
	(*a*) Trees/palms	Once every three months
	(*b*) Shrubs/ground covers	Monthly
	(*c*) Grass	Once every three months
5.	Loosening of soil	Monthly
6.	Control of pest by applying appropriate insecticides	Fortnightly
7.	Control of disease by applying appropriate fungicides.	Monthly, increasing the frequency to fortnightly during rainy season
8.	Grass cutting	Fortnightly
9.	Pruning and shaping trees/palms	Once every six months for small and low sagging branches
10.	Staking	As and when required.
11.	Trimming shrubs/ground covers	Monthly or as when required

7. Clean-Up Works:

There shall be areas designated by landscape architect for the contractor to carry out clean-up works. These shall include the following:

(*a*) Removal of dead and/or overhanging branches of existing trees, palms, shrubs and groundcovers.

(*b*) Removal of any garbage and unsightly foreign materials.

(*c*) Removal of dead vines and plant materials.

The contractor shall prevent damages to the existing plant materials, identified to be conserved. The plant materials that are to be conserved if damaged beyond use during the clean-up operations, the contractor shall be liable to replace the plant materials at their own expense.

8. Restoration:

The contractor is responsible for the use of all materials, labour and equipments and any injury to the plant material, labour and equipment will be repaired or the same replaced by the contractor at his own expense.

9. Completion:

On completion, the ground shall be formed over and left tidy.

J. Service Utilities In Landscape

1. Designed integration of structures and elements related to external services (underground and over ground utilities) with landscape is most essential for any outdoor space.

The following services are generally subject of design co-ordination work for external areas:

2. Storm water drainage :
   1. Storm water network;
   2. Open drain and swale;
   3. Subsurface drainage system;
   4. Catch basin and manholes;
   5. Culvert and bridge;
   6. Percolation pits;
   7. Water harvesting units;
   8. Retention walls and tanks;
   9. Connection of all service lines up to out-designed integration of external services networks and fall; and elements in the landscape proposal; and
   10. Other related structures.

3. Sewage disposal system:
   1. Sewerage network;
   2. Manholes, inspection chambers and grease trap;
   3. Septic tank, soak-pits, sewage treatment plant and root zone unit;
   4. Solid waste management units;
   5. Connection of all service lines up to out-fall; and
   6. Other related structures.

4. Water supply
   1. Water supply network;
   2. Inspection chamber and valve chamber;
   3. Water tank and treatment plant;
   4. Tube well, bore well and associated pump houses, etc; and
   5. Service lines, elements associated with water features and pools.

5. Fire lines:
   1. Yard hydrant lines;
   2. Yard or fire hydrants and hose reel box;
   3. Fire water tank and pumps; and

4. Inspection chamber and valve chamber.

6. Electrical works:
   1. Electrical network;
   2. Light fixtures for road, pedestrian paths; special landscape features and building facade;
   3. Inspection chambers, junction boxes and feeder pillars;
   4. Electric poles, high voltage lines and towers;
   5. Transformer, substation and distribution box; and
   6. Other related structures.
7. Telephone and under-ground cable network:
   1. Telephone network;
   2. Inspection chambers;
   3. Telephone poles, transmission towers; and
   4. Other related structures.
8. Fuel and gas line:
   1. Supply network;
   2. Inspection chamber and valve chamber;
   3. Fuel tank and gas tank; and
   4. Other related structures.
9. The following guidelines shall be applied for the designed integration of external services networks and elements in the landscape proposal:
   1. The manholes and inspection chamber covers for all external services should be adequately designed for the live load (pedestrian or vehicular) and the top finish level has to be in alignment or flushed with the pavement or finished ground level. The alignment of these structures should be such that it is in geometric perpendicular or parallel with adjacent building or landscape lines. This would facilitate easy and unobstructed movement for pedestrians and increase the accessibility for wheelchair users in public place and also aid the landscape geometry to be maintained.
   2. Fire hydrants should be prominently located and integrated with the landscape. Aesthetically designed fire hose cabinet with clear access as per statutory norms for fire safety, to be located in geometric relation with adjacent building or landscape lines. These structures should not be a hindrance to vehicular or pedestrian movement.
   3. Irrigation hydrants should be unobtrusively located and generally at the edge of shrub planting and additionally in close proximity to a drainage chamber or catch basin to avoid waterlog. Hydrants should not be located inside the chamber to minimize waterlog from leaking pipes causing various health related hazards. Hydrants should be located 200 mm above the ground level.

4. Landscape lighting is a specialized activity and illumination consultant or designer should develop the landscape lighting plan taking into consideration energy saving measures, safety aspects, lighting pollution and illumination level. Light fixtures are an important part of street furniture and it is advisable to use pole mounted light fixtures for public landscape than bollards that are prone to vandalism, and damage.
5. Water body and fountains in public spaces should have filtration facility to avoid health hazards related to stagnant water. The piping should be concealed and the pump room, balancing tank and all other service structures to be designed as an integral part of landscape.
6. Storage facilities for inflammable liquid fuel and gas should be designed as an integral part of the landscape and should be housed in designed enclosures taking into consideration all statutory norms these structures are subjected to g) All underground service lines have to be well coordinated and stacked appropriately in the design stage to avoid overlaps and marked with indicators above the ground for ease in maintenance and servicing. Underground service stacks should be generally aligned in soft areas with no tree plantation; this would facilitate easy maintenance without disrupting the hard surface.
7. Designed facade for service structures that are above the ground in external areas is advisable so as to assist in developing aesthetically pleasing exterior environment. Such structures should be designed in a modular way so that it would be part of the street furniture.

10. Paved Surfaces in External Areas:

The paved areas that are used for movement of vehicles, pedestrians and wheel chair users in outdoor environment have to be designed to facilitate easy accessibility, with well drained surface, and good visual clues achieved with varied colour and texture of finishing materials. The following guidelines may be applied for the design of paved outdoor spaces:

1. Roads should provide clear access to fire fighting vehicles, ambulance, sanitation vehicles, etc and also allow safe movement for vehicles, pedestrians and wheel chair users.
2. Kerbs are required on all roads to adequately control drainage within the road, prevent moisture from entering the sub-grade, separate the road from the pedestrian area, and provide adequate lateral support for the pavement structure.
3. Pedestrian circulation path consists of sidewalks, wheelchair ramp, and landings. Pathways of minimum width 1.50 m required along the length of road for any public or private building where pedestrian traffic is excepted.
4. Path way should be physically separated by means of kerb, graded separation, barrier, railing, or other means. The cross slope of sidewalk will not exceed two percent. The longitudinal slope of path should not exceed 1 in 20, unless the longitudinal slope of the road exceeds this maximum, in that case the standards which conform to a ramp should be applied.
5. Benches, shelters, poles, signs, bus stops, etc should be located on edge of the sidewalk with clear minimum width of 1.20 m for circulation path.
6. All ramps should have minimum width of 1.20 m, excluding edge protection. The cross slope of ramp should not exceed 1 in 50. and longitudinal slope of ramp should not exceed 1 in 12. All ramps should have an unobstructed level landing both at top and bottom of the ramp. The landing should have the minimum width as the ramp. The landing should be minimum 1.50 m in length. Any ramp beside the road should be located in such a way so that vehicles cannot park blocking the access.

7. Handrail would be required for any ramp with greater vertical height than 300 mm to prevent pedestrians and wheelchair users slipping from the ramp. The height of the top handrail should be 900 mm from the top surface of the ramp. The ramp surface should be rough finished. All ramp and landing should be designed so that water does not collect on the surface of the ramp or landing.
8. Stone not less than 40 mm in thickness should be used as paving finish in external areas. Adequate slope and drainage facility to be considered for all external paved surface integrating it with the pavement design.
9. Smooth finish is not recommended for external areas except to convey any design concept.
10. Change in levels and steps may be depicted in different texture or colour as a visual clue.
11. Street Furniture:

The design elements for outdoor spaces may be classified under the following categories:

1. Pavement and other pedestrian movement spaces, covering
    1. Footpath with heavy pedestrian traffic,
    2. Footpath with light pedestrian traffic,
    3. Plaza and public assembly spaces,
    4. Kerb to footpath, and
    5. Steps and ramps.
2. Parking and vehicular movement corridor, covering
    1. Parking unit,
    2. Median and road divider,
    3. Road marking, and
    4. Speed breaker.
3. Traffic management units, covering
    1. Bollards,
    2. Barriers,
    3. Crash guard,
    4. Gate/Access control,
    5. Vehicular height restrictors, and
    6. Traffic separators.
4. Outdoor public conveniences, covering
    1. Seating,

2. Drinking fountains, and
3. Toilet/Wash rooms.

5. Shelter and kiosks, covering
   1. Bus shelters,
   2. Police booth,
   3. Telephone booth,
   4. Milk booth/Food stall,
   5. Florist,
   6. Information desk, and
   7. Snack and coffee stall.

6. Outdoor illumination, covering
   1. Street light,
   2. Facade light, and
   3. Bollard light.

7. Tree protection units, covering
   1. Tree guard,
   2. Tree grate, and
   3. Planter.

8. Garbage collection units, covering
   1. Litter bin, and
   2. Spittoons.

9. Service utilities, relating to
   1. Water supply network,
   2. Storm water network,
   3. Sewerage network,
   4. Electrical network,
   5. Telephone lines,
   6. Cable e-net, and
   7. Gas.

12. Display and Signage:

Location of the street furniture has to coordinate with the traffic flow pattern of vehicles and pedestrians and external services.

(Source: National Building Code 2005 of India)

EXERCISE

1. What are the contents of 'Landscape development permit'?
2. What are 'Landscape Plan Contents and Specifications'?
3. What kind of protection is needed during landscape construction?
4. What are the various measures to be adopted for 'Soil and Water conservation'?
5. What measures are to be taken for conservation and re-use of water for irrigation?
6. Explain the various earth slopes and grading requirements?
7. What are the major planting design considerations?
8. Explain the specifications for planting works?
9. What are the various service utilities and how do you integrate them in landscape design?

12

Landscape Design Terminology

Acidity: Acidity is the characteristic of soils having a pH level of less than 7. Acidity can be raised by using commercial fertilizers containing ammonium-N. Plants of alkaline soil may perform poorly in acidic soils.

Aerobic: It means an organism, which needs atmospheric oxygen to thrive. In landscaping and gardening, it is used for compost bins. Well-designed and maintained compost bins promote an environment for aerobic organisms to thrive. Aerobic organisms are an important ingredient in good compost. The material in a compost bin will not work properly without them.

Aesthetic: It means visually pleasing. Aesthetics means the study of the appreciation of beauty. Landscape design is concerned both with aesthetic and functional elements of landscaping.

Agronomy: Agronomy is both the study and the management of the science of land, usually agricultural or rural land.

Alkalinity: Alkalinity is the characteristic of soils with a pH level greater than 7, which is suitable for plants that thrive in an alkaline soil. Apply lime, if soil pH needs to be raised.

Anaerobic: "Anaerobic" is often used to such organisms living in a compost bin and influencing the quality of its decomposition. It also refers to the conditions under which such organisms thrive. Anaerobic organisms like bacteria can live in the absence of atmospheric oxygen.

Annual plants: Annual plants are those that last but a year in their native climates. They will bloom completely and die out in the winter time or once the bloom of flowers is over. Annual plants last only one year, however their color makes them well worth the investment.

Aquatic Plants: Aquatic plants are marine plants, which grow extremely well in fresh water. They are used on ponds to add greenery. There are different types of aquatic plants.

Arbor: Arbors are open frameworks made of wood or lattice intended to create a shady area within a garden or landscape. Arbors are often made of rustic work or latticework which serves as a trellis for climbers or creepers.

Arboriculture: Arboriculture is the art, science, technology and business of tree care. Arboriculture is practiced by arborists. Arborists are trained to promote tree health, detect tree problems and take measures to correct them.

Arborist: Arborists are professionals who practice arboriculture. Certified arborists are accredited by the International Society of Arboriculture.

Balled and burlapped: Balled and burlapped plants are transplants shipped to the consumer after being planted, dug up and wrapped. 'Balled' refers to the root ball which has been dug up, while 'burlapped' refers to the wrapping material used for transporting tree and shrub deliveries. The burlap is fastened with string, wire or twine. Wire and rot-resistant burlap needs to be removed when planting.

Bare-root: Bare root plants are plants shipped to the consumer without being planted in soil making them inactive. For example Rose bushes are sometimes shipped as bare root plants.

Basket weave brick pattern: When laying bricks various designs or paving patterns can be used. One of these paving patterns is known as "basket weave" pattern. Another popular brick pattern is called "herringbone." The basket weave pattern is essentially composed of pairs of bricks.

Bedding Plants: Bedding plants massed with others to produce maximum visual appeal. A landscape designer can arrange each bedding plant in relation to the accompanying annuals, perennials, shrubs and trees.

Biodegradable: It means the capacity of being decomposed back into the soil by biological agents, especially bacteria. The term "Biodegradable" is often used for items to be disposed off. Environmentally conscious landscaping takes into account whether materials are biodegradable or not. For example, plastic might be rejected as a mulch material because it is not biodegradable.

Broadleaf: It is often used for lawn and garden weeds to separate them from other weeds for categorization. It also refers to garden shrubs and trees having "regular" leaves.

Buck: It refers to cutting a felled tree into shorter lengths. For example; for log cabin construction, cut a tree down, then "buck" it into the lengths required for construction purposes.

Bud: A thick branch containing an embryonic leaf, leaf cluster or flower.

Bulb: A fleshy underground plant structure that contains the nutrients, energy and seed to produce a plant. Bulbs are typically buried in the ground at least one season before they emerge. Daffodils, lilies and tulips are common examples of bulbs

Cabling: In 'Cabling method' cables are used to stabilize an established tree, which is growing in a sustainable manner. Cabling is often employed by arborists to save a specimen tree. If cabling isn't done properly, it can result in 'girdling'. An arborist knows how to position the cables. Sometimes, cabling is used to save a tree with a split trunk. Another use of cabling is to support a large branch growing at an awkward angle. Cabling is achieved by drilling holes in the trunks or branches of the tree. Support in cabling is totally above-ground.

Cambium: It is the layer of cells lying between the wood and bark of a stem from which new bark and wood cells originate. Climbing trees with spikes damages the cambium.

Cascade: A cascade is a display of falling water arranged in levels or stages by using an informal rock formation, steps or some other means creating the cascading effect.

Chilling: Chilling requirements for fruit trees, nut trees, bulb plants, shrubs and other plants are measured in terms of the total hours needed during a dormant or winter period when the temperature is below 45ºF and above 32ºF. It helps in normal growth and bloom in the succeeding growing season.

Climbers: Plants that climb on their own are called as 'Climbers'. Some climbers wind their way around supports. Other climbers climb by using tendrils or some other method. Climbers are often supplied with arbors to climb. Vine plants can be subdivided into the general categories of climbers and creepers.

Clump: Clumps are clusters of plant life. They are planted strategically in gardens to achieve some type of picturesque visual effect.

Cold frame: Cold frames are unheated outdoor landscape structures composed of a wooden or concrete framework and covered with glass or plastic. Cold frames are used for the process of hardening off seedlings. They can also help extending the growing season and sheltering plants from cold or frost.

Commensal: Commensal is applied to pests which share the same food as another. Commensal is often used for rodent pests of the landscape, which share human food. House mice and rats are the chief commensal rodents. Commensal pests are prevented by keeping food in well-sealed containers. It is preferable to take preventive measures against rodents and other pests.

Companion planting: It is the practice of planting one plant in proximity to another due to the benefits it adds on the "companion plant." For example, gardeners often put side by side certain plants because one will have insect-repelling qualities that benefit the other eliminating the need to use chemical pesticides. Sometimes, one plant can even serve as 'mulch' for another plant.

Complete fertilizers: Complete fertilizers contain nitrogen, phosphorus and potassium. These three are important fertilizer ingredients. A fertilizer listed as "10-10-10" is a complete fertilizer, whereas a fertilizer listed as "10-0-10" is not a complete fertilizer. The middle zero indicates the absence of phosphorus in the fertilizer.

Composite Decking: Composite decking is an artificially created material, unlike wood, is resistant to fading and mold or mildew.

Compost bins: Compost bins are structures built to house compost. Compost bins facilitate the decomposition of organic matter through proper aeration and moisture retention. Ideal conditions are produced with proper combination of air and moisture for the activity of aerobic organisms, which transform the organic materials into compost.

Compost: It is a mixture of decaying organic matter used to improve soil structure and provide nutrients. Compost is placed in a "compost pile", which may be stored in a structure called a "compost bin." The composting process is the result of the activity of aerobic organisms. Compost is the basis of organic gardening.

Conifers: It is an arboricultural term meaning a cone-bearer. Trees which are conifers reproduce by forming a cone than a flower as a container for their seeds.

Contour Lines: They are used for depicting and measuring slopes and drainage points. Contour lines are also map lines that connect two or more points along the same ground elevation.

Contour: Contour refers to the shape and form of the land.

Control joints: Control joints are grooves inserted into a concrete surface to control cracking. This groove is an intentional crack placed in the concrete to prevent concrete cracking in an uncontrolled manner. Haphazard cracks can be avoided by placing control joints in concrete before it cures. A mason can cut an even control joint, which will be aesthetically pleasing. Control joints can be cut into existing concrete surfaces using a saw with a masonry blade.

Core aeration: It is the process of mechanically removing plugs of soil and thatch from a lawn. Core aeration reduces soil compaction.

Corms: In some plants, a bulbous stem growing underground storing food for potential roots, leaves and flowers is called a "corm".

Cotyledon leaves: They are the leaves of the embryo of a seed plant, which remain in the seed or emerge, enlarge and become green upon germination. Cotyledon leaves are also called "false leaves" in contrast to the "true leaves" which develop later.

Cover crops: Cover crops are planted for soil erosion control, weed control and improving soil quality. A cover crop is usually ploughed before the next food crop is planted. The choice between various cover crops is influenced by aesthetics because the cover crop is taking the place of garden plants in between growing seasons. When plants are chosen to cover the ground based mainly on aesthetic considerations, they are no longer considered "cover crops" but they are classified as groundcovers.

Creepers: Creepers are vine plants artificially guided and secured to a support to grow upright.

Cultivar: It is a cultivated variety of a plant which has been intentionally selected for specific desirable characteristics such as the color and form of the flower, yield of the crop, disease resistance, etc. When spread correctly, the plants of a particular cultivar retain their special characteristics.

Deadhead: To 'deadhead' plants means to remove their spent flowers. Deadheading promotes more flowering on the plants for that year than would occur. For soft plants, deadhead can be done by hand. In case of some other plants, scissors or pruners are required. It is a good idea to deadhead annual plants to achieve maximal landscaping with four-season interest. Deadheading gives them the chance to continue blooming throughout the summer. Without deadheading, some annual flowers will die prematurely robbing the landscape of the color they can provide. Short blooming season of some perennials can be extended by deadheading. 'Deadhead' and 'pinch' are very similar terms. People also deadhead plants to keep ugly, dried-up flowers from marring the appearance of a planting bed.

Deciduous: It means a plant sheds its foliage at the end of the growing season. It is used with reference to trees and shrubs. The best-known deciduous trees are the fall foliage trees.

Deck girder: A deck girder is a board or a composite of boards serving as a supporting beam for the deck joists.

Deck joists: Deck joists are boards forming a structural framework to the stability of a deck. The top of the deck joists form the surface for fixing the flooring of the deck using nails or screws.

Decking materials: Decking materials form the flooring of a deck. The deck flooring is the uppermost element of the deck structure. Deck flooring or decking is supported from the bottom to the top by concrete footings, concrete piers, posts, girder, header board and joists.

Decking: Decking is the construction of decks made of either wood or composite materials to create a recreational area near or above the ground.

Dethatching: The mechanical removal of the layer of dead turf grass tissue from a lawn, which is known as 'thatch' is called 'Dethatching'.

Dioecious: If male and female reproductive organs are carried on separate individual plants of the same species, then that plant species is known as 'Dioecious'. When a plant species is dioecious, at least one male plant must be present in a group for the fruit-bearing female plants to be pollinated. By contrast, 'Monoecious' plants have unisexual reproductive organs or flowers, with the organs or flowers of both sexes borne on a single plant.

Dormancy: It means temporary reduction or stop of a plant growth during winter in the temperate zone. Dormancy is also applied to the land. The land is said to be in a state of dormancy during periods when no primary crop is being grown. However, a secondary crop may be grown on the land during periods of dormancy.

Down: Down refers to an undulating upland plain, which is completely devoid of any trees.

Drainage: It involves the removal of excess water from a landscape to improve the soil structure either mechanically through the use of some type of system or naturally with surface ditches.

Drip irrigation: Drip irrigation system uses low volumes of low-pressure water discharged drip by drip at the base of a plant. This is the most economical and efficient way to use water.

Dry wall: When stones are not held together by mortar, then it is known as 'Dry wall'. It can be a stone wall or brick wall. Dry-wall construction requires precision in the way stones or bricks are stacked because proper placement alone keeps the wall intact.

Ecology: Ecology is a branch of biology that focuses on the relationships between living things and the environment in which they live.

Ecosystem: An ecosystem is comprised of animals, plants and microorganisms. All of them function together interdependently within the habitat.

Edging plant: They are compact plants put together with similar plants to form a border in a landscape design.

Edging: Edging is a dividing line of demarcation creating visual interest in a landscape by separating one section from another.

Espalier: When a tree, shrub or vine is trained to grow on a single plane without deviating, then it is known as the "espalier" style. The plane is often defined by a wall or fence. Young plants are trained on wires running along the wall or fence. The later "espalier" is pruned to keep its growth parallel to the wall or fence. Sometimes, the trellis formed by the wire is referred as "espalier.

Evergreen: It means having foliage, which retains its color throughout the year without changing color according to the seasons. Trees and shrubs can be classified as either evergreen or deciduous.

Finials: Finials are the small, ornamental, terminal features at the top of a gable, fence post, lamp, lamppost or stone wall. Their job is aesthetic, giving a finishing touch to a hardscape feature.

Float: A float is a spreading tool used in masonry with a handle fastened to a flat piece. Floats are used to finish a concrete surface.

Flower nodes: Places from which leaves or branches grow on a flower stem are called as 'Flower nodes'. Similarly the places from which leaves, buds or other branches grow are called 'nodes'.

Forcing: It is the process of making a plant bloom before its natural season.

Friable soil: It is a soil which has the crumbly texture ideal for the root growth of plants. Such friable soil is usually a 'loam'.

Fumigate: Fumigate means to use a toxic gas to control tunneling rodent pests.

Gazebo: It is a small roofed structure set up for outdoor dining and entertaining. It is often octagonal in shape with open, screened or latticework sides.

Girdling: In arboricultural terminology, girdling is the choking of a tree branch through a material applied by a human or a vine that has vigorously enwrapped a tree.

Glade: Glades are open, grassy areas surrounded completely by woods.

Grade: Grade refers to the way a plot of land slopes.

Grafting: Grafting is the uniting of a shoot or bud with an established plant, either by insertion or by placing them in close contact. Grafting is a common procedure in the development of fruit tree stock.

Green manure crops: These are cover crops planted when a garden is in a state of dormancy. They are not grown for their own sake but to be ploughed or tilled before the regular growing season. Like compost, green manure crops serve as a soil amendment.

Green Wall: A green wall may be freestanding or a part of a structure, which is either totally or partially covered with some type of vegetation grown with soil or some kind of inorganic growing medium. There are two types of green walls. They are 'Green facades' and 'Living walls'. Green facades are made from climbing plants such as vines, which grow directly on the wall. Living walls comprise of components like modular panels, plastic containers, an irrigation system, the growing medium and the vegetation.

Greenbelt: Greenbelts are strips of either agricultural or outlying areas of land which are usually planted with trees and used to separate or encircle urban areas.

Grotto: Grottos are intricately decorated underground passages containing running rills and pools of water combined together to create a mysterious effect. A grotto is usually adorned with pieces of stone, broken shells and mirrors.

Ground Water: Ground water is the accumulation of rain and melted snow in porous rocks located within the earth.

Groundcovers: Groundcovers are low-lying plants chosen for aesthetic considerations with minimal maintenance. The initial cost will be high than for sowing grass seed to cover large area of ground on the landscape. However, they may save money in the long run.

Gutter: Also known as downspouts, rainspouts, troughs and spouts. Gutters are installed under a roof's eaves for draining rainwater

Hardening off: Hardening off is the process of preparing plants started indoors to adapt to environmental conditions to be faced when permanently moved outdoors. The process of hardening off plants involves a transitional period, when plants are left outside during daylight only and in an area shaded and protected from wind. Watering is reduced during the hardening off period. Gradually, the plant is allowed exposure to an increasing amount of sunlight and allowed to stay out later. Plants will be negatively affected by the sudden shock of exposure to day-time sunrays and night-time coolness without allowing plants to harden off.

Header board: This term is used in deck construction. The deck is usually tied into the house structurally, when it projects out from a house. A header board is bolted to the house to achieve this.

Heading-back: Heading-back is an act of pruning the growth of head of a plant. Heading back is categorized into "topping" and "pollarding." Topping is done on large old trees as an inexpensive alternative than full removal. Pollarding is done for aesthetic reasons. Pollarding begins when a tree is young and continues throughout the life of the tree.

Herbaceous: An herbaceous plant has leaves and stems that die down at the end of the growing season to the soil level. They have no persistent woody stem above ground. Herbaceous plants may be annuals, biennials or perennials.

Hermitage: Hermitage is a small, rustic garden building used as a place to enjoy the beauty of the surrounding nature.

Herringbone: It is the name of a pattern used often in brick laying. Herringbone stamped concrete patterns can imitate such brick designs. The herringbone design is sometimes described as a "zigzag" pattern.

Horticulture: Horticulture is the art and science of cultivating fruits, vegetables, flowers or ornamental plants. Horticulture involves five areas of study. They are:

1. Floriculture (production and marketing of floral crops)
2. Landscape horticulture (production, marketing and maintenance of landscape plants)
3. Olericulture (production and marketing of vegetables)
4. Pomology (includes production and marketing of fruits)
5. Post-harvest physiology (maintaining quality and preventing spoilage of horticultural crops)

Humus: It is an organic matter partly or wholly decomposed. When the decomposition of humus is expedited to use it as a soil improvement, it is almost equivalent to compost. A large admixture of humus to soil can make it friable.

Hybrid plants: Hybrid plants are produced by instilling the pistil of one species with the pollen of another.

Impervious: Impervious means incapable of being penetrated. Soil can become impervious through foot traffic, construction or other activities.

Indigenous plants: Indigenous plants are the native plants of the soil. Sometimes they are allowed to co-exist with lawn grass, foreign ground covers or garden plants.

Integrated pest management (IPM): It is the management of pest problems involving use of control measures in an integrated manner. The core idea is to take preventive steps to rule out a pest problem instead of eradicating them later.

Invasive plants: Plant species showing a tendency to spread out of control are called as 'Invasive plants'. These plants introduced from other regions spread like wildfire in their new habitats. Their tendency to spread may be due to the fact that the insects and diseases of their native lands are often absent in their new homes. Invasive plants produce a monoculture discouraging the growth of other plant varieties. Exotic invasive plants often force out indigenous plants. It is necessary to act aggressively to eradicate invasive plants like weeds in the lawn or garden.

Invertebrates: They are animals without a backbone like insects. Animal pests are usually categorized as invertebrate pests or vertebrate pests.

Japanese bonsai: Japanese Bonsai is the historic art of dwarfing trees by careful root and stem pruning with root restriction. Bonsai means "potted plant" because Japanese bonsai trees are often kept in containers. Junipers and other needle-bearing evergreens are the most popular bonsai plants.

Jointed plant: It means the plant possesses a stem with nodes.

Jointer: It is a tool used to make control joints on a newly poured concrete surface.

Knot gardens: They are symmetrically designed gardens by the precise use of edging plants. Knot gardens are particularly associated with the grand English estates.

Land Use: Land use denotes the designated use or activity on a specific site of land.

Landscape Architect: A landscape architect is a professional responsible for the designing, planning and management of an outdoor landscape space. Landscape architects projects may range from an entire ecosystem to a much smaller residential site.

Landscape architecture: It is a profession of designing a landscape for aesthetic or practical purposes. Landscape architecture calls for a broader skill and carries greater responsibility.

Landscape Designer: Landscape designers work to design and create different types of landscapes, but they are not registered or licensed to hold title of a landscape architect.

Landscape gardening: Landscape gardening is the decoration of land by planting trees and shrubs and designing gardens.

Latticework: Latticework is an open framework made of strips of metal, wood or similar material overlaid in a regular crisscross pattern. Latticework is often seen as a component of porches or decks. Traditionally, trellises were made of latticework.

Lawn thatch: It is the layer of dead turf-grass tissue between the green vegetation and the soil surface to be removed, which is known as 'dethatching', to maintain lawn health. Lawn thatch is derived from stems, leaves, stolons, rhizomes and roots.

Leader: It is the primary or top stem of a plant. Where multiples are present as the potential leader, select one pruning away the rest to channelize energy into the selected branch.

Limbing: It means removing unwanted limbs from a tree. Large support branches hanging dangerously over a house often require 'limbing'. Such limbing work is best performed by arborists.

Lime: Lime is a rock powder used to raise the pH of soils high in acidity. An application of lime makes the soil more alkaline and useful for battling outdoor pet odors.

Living mulches: They are cover crop plants planted around and in between the primary plants to control weeds, prevent erosion, help water penetration and improve the soil. It can also be referred to groundcovers planted for weed control. Living mulches serve a role similar to that of more conventional mulches. Living mulch plants are sometimes used in companion planting.

Loamy soil: It is a friable soil having a proper mixture of clay, sand and humus suitable for growing plants.

Masonry: Masonry construction is achieved through the use of units of various natural or artificial mineral products such as stone, brick or concrete. The word, masonry can be used to the craftsmanship or to the finished product.

Microclimate: A 'microclimate' is the climate of a specific place within an area, when compared to the climate of the entire area or the 'macroclimate'.

Monoculture: Monoculture means the use of land for growing only one type of plant or the plant culture. The practice of monoculture can sometimes be responsible for the spread of plant diseases. Sometimes monoculture is unplanned, it occurs when an invasive plant forces out other plants and dominates an area of the landscape.

Monoecious: It is a plant bearing both male and female reproductive organs.

Mortar: Mortar is a masonry product composed of cement and sand. Concrete contains coarse aggregate bound together by the cement. Concrete can stand alone, while mortar is used to hold brick or stone together.

Mortared walls: Stone walls can be classified into two categories. When the stones are held together by mortar, then they are called 'mortared walls'. When the stones are free-standing, then they are called 'dry walls'.

Mulch: Mulch is a covering placed around plants to prevent the growth of weeds. Mulch reduces erosion and water loss, and regulates soil temperature. After decomposition mulches serve as soil amendments.

Native Species: Plant life, which is indigenous or native to a specific ecosystem or natural habitat, is known as 'Native species'

Naturalized plants: These are plants established as a part of the flora of a place other than their place of origin. When a plant naturalizes in an area, it can be either good or bad depending upon that particular naturalized plant.

Neutral pH: If soil is neither acidic nor alkaline, then it has a neutral pH. A soil with a neutral pH has a pH value of 7.

Nitrogen fixers: Nitrogen fixers are cover crops whose roots are colonized by certain bacteria which extract nitrogen from the air and convert into a form required for their growth. When the bacteria are done with this nitrogen, it becomes available to the cover crop. While tilling the cover crop, the nitrogen is made available to the plants.

NPK: NPK is a word form for nitrogen, phosphorus and potassium. These three nutrients compose a complete fertilizer. NPK is printed on bags of fertilizer.

Open-pollinated plants: These are plants which are pollinated without human agency.

Parkway: A parkway is a stretch of road laid through a garden containing a median strip along with plant life along the side of the road.

Perennial plants: Perennials have a life cycle of more than 3 years, as opposed to 'annual plants' of one year and 'biennial plants' of two years.

Pergolas: Pergola design and arbor design are similar. Garden arbors are simple and relatively small structures. They are arched often at the top. Pergolas are larger structures with architectural treatment. The primary difference is that an arbor is a free-standing structure, whereas a pergola is a long linear structure over a garden pathway.

Pistillate: Pistillate means 'bearing pistils'. Pistillate plant parts are 'female'. They bear ovules and produce seeds.

Plant taxonomy: It is a system of classification used by botanists and horticulturists. The plant taxonomy was developed by Linnaeus (1707-1778). Linnaeus simplified plant taxonomy through the 'binomial' system. Linnaeus system uses one Latin name to indicate the genus and another to indicate the specific name. The genus and name together comprise the species. For example bittersweet nightshade is classified as *Solanum dulcamara*, where the first Latin name is for the genus (nightshade) and the second is for the specific name (bittersweet).

The species is a subset of the genus. The genus begins with a capital. The name with lower-case. Both are italicized.

While translating from Latin, the order of the names is reversed, putting the name before the genus.

Sometimes in plant taxonomy, a third name is used describing the variation within a species. Normally this third name is a cultivar appearing in quotation marks.

Sometimes yet another word is added after the genus and name, which is neither italicized nor set off by quotation marks. It is the name of the person who first described the plant. When the name is shortened as 'L', it stands for 'Linnaeus'.

Genus followed by the letter 'x', followed by a name, indicates a hybrid plant.

Pollarding trees: Pollarding a tree means cutting a tree back nearly to the trunk to produce a dense mass of branches for aesthetic purposes. Pollarding begins on young trees and repeated throughout the life of the tree.

Procumbent plants: They are plants which trail along the ground. It is used for plants which cannot grow upright unless aided.

Reforestation: Reforestation is the act of replanting existing woodlands or forests depleted by human use. Reforestation is a solution to important problems like global warming, reducing the number of endangered species, saving the rainforests and protecting ecosystems.

Retaining Walls: Retaining walls are structures built to support soil or water to prevent advancing forward.

Retention pond: It is a hole dug to capture and hold surface drainage water.

Revegetation: Revegetation means rebuilding and replanting soil on landscape which has been disturbed or damaged because of wildfires, mining, flooding, and other natural or man-made causes.

Rhizomes: Rhizomes are horizontal underground stems which strike new roots into the soil. These new roots shoot new stems out of their nodes up to the surface. It represents a form of plant reproduction activity. The uncontrollable nature of many invasive plants is due to the strength of their rhizomes.

Rootstock: It means the root or part of a root used for plant propagation. The rootstock is a part of a grafted plant which supplies the roots in the process of grafting.

Scaffold branches: A scaffold branch is one of the main limbs radiating from the trunk of a tree. All subordinate branches stem from the scaffold branches.

Scion: The scion is the detached branch containing buds from a woody plant used in grafting. The scion is grafted onto the rootstock.

Screed: A screed is a straight board used to even off the surface of sand or freshly poured concrete.

Sheet composting: It is a technique of spreading organic materials over a garden before they have thoroughly decomposed. Those who cannot manage a compost bin for decomposing organic materials employ the technique of sheet composting. Sheet composting involves spreading a thin layer of organic materials, such as leaves, over a garden area. The materials are then tilled in with a hoe, spade, garden fork or rotary tiller. To help decomposition, materials should be shredded or chopped prior to layering.

Shrubs: Shrubs are low woody plants with multiple branches or stems from the base, which attain a height of 15 feet or less at maturity. A planting of shrubs is called 'shrubbery'.

Site Planning: Site planning is an organizational phase of the entire landscape design process. Beginning with site analysis, site planning includes number of aspects of landscaping such as drainage issues, privacy, security and soil conditions.

Soil amendment: Soil amendments are elements added to the soil like compost, peat moss or fertilizer to improve its capacity to support plant life. While fertilizer improves soil by adding nutrients only, soil amendments such as peat moss improve soil by making its texture or drainage more conducive to plant health.

Soil compaction: This term is used to soil which suffers from excessive water runoff and poor conditions for plant rooting. Soil compaction in a lawn can be corrected mechanically through core aeration. People often employ garden tillers to break up compacted soil for a new garden. Earthworms can help avoid a recurrence of soil compaction. Compaction occurs under anaerobic conditions in compost bins. Turning a compost pile frequently is one way to avoid such compaction.

Soil pH: Soil pH is the measure of the acidity or alkalinity of a soil. A pH value 7 indicates neutral soils, increase indicates rising alkalinity and decrease indicates rising acidity. The soil pH scale normally ranges from 0 to 14. Soil pH is not fixed, it can be altered. To reduce soil pH, apply commercial fertilizers containing sulfur / ammonium. To increase soil pH, apply lime.

Specimen plants: 'Specimen plants' are grown in a lawn or garden for aesthetic effect. Specimen plants can serve as focal points in landscape design. An example of a specimen plant is a flowering tree, which has a prominent spot reserved for it.

Staminate: A flower that lacks stamens is 'pistillate' or female. One that lacks pistils is 'staminate' or male. When the same plant bears unisexual flowers of both sexes, it is said to be 'monoecious'.

Stolons: Stolons are branches which bend to the ground or grow horizontally above the ground producing roots and branches at the nodes. In contrast to stolons, rhizomes live underground.

Systemic poisons: They are insecticides mixed in a plant's soil and drawn up by its roots to its stem and leaves, where they will be absorbed by the pest to kill. The use of systemic poisons is preferable to spraying. By the time spraying is carried out, significant plant damage may already have occurred.

Tendrils: Tendrils are twisting threadlike structures. True climbers grasp an object for support. Vines with tendrils climb on their own. In some cases, vines are tied to arbors, pergolas, latticework or other structures even if they have tendrils to climb precisely in the desired direction.

Topiary: Topiary means the art of pruning of live shrubs or trees into decorative shapes. The results of such pruning are known as 'topiaries'.

Topography: Topography generally refers to the setting of the land like the way it slopes as well as its drainage patterns. It is also the science of creating charts and maps used to represent the surface features (natural and man-made) of an area.

Topping trees: Topping trees means cutting trees back nearly to the trunk. Topping is used as a less expensive alternative to the full removal of large old trees. In contrast, 'pollarding' begins on young trees for aesthetic purpose, not for utilitarian purpose. Pollarding is an ongoing process, whereas topping is a one-time action.

Trees: A tree is a woody plant with one main trunk and a distinct and elevated head. Trees generally reach a height of 13 feet or more without cutting.

Variegated: It is used for a flower or a leaf, which is two-toned: blotched or bordered with a lighter color than the whole color of a flower or leaf. It is also used to a whole plant bearing variegated leaves or flowers.

Vernalisation: It is process, where plants are prepared for flowering through exposure to cold temperatures. Vernalization is achieved not only through human handling, but also occurs naturally. A chilling requirement is a standard to be met for vernalization to occur. With chilling requirements, the chance of a plant flowering in a particular region can be quantified. There is a need to draw a distinction between 'vernalization' and 'forcing'. Both words mean coaxing plants into blooming earlier in the season than would happen in nature. In 'forcing' flowers into bloom by cutting means providing plants artificially with warmer temperatures to bloom. In contrast 'vernalization' is all about cold temperatures.

Vertebrate animals: Animals with a backbone are vertebrates. Vertebrate animals are mammals, birds, fish, reptiles and amphibians. Animal garden pests are usually classified into vertebrate or invertebrate pests. The vertebrate animals most likely to damage plants are mammals like deer, rabbits and rodents.

Vines: A plant is a vine, if its stem is too weak to support its vertical growth. It will either seek such support from other sources or simply trail along the ground. Vines are classified as either climbers or creepers.

Weep hole: Weep hole is a small drainage outlet at the base of a retaining wall allowing water to seep out. It prevents the build up of water pressure which may damage the wall.

Wood burls: Wood burls are large, rounded branches on the trunk or branch of a tree. Irritants such as bacteria are the cause of wood burls. They are often used decoratively as a veneer in woodcraft. Wood burls are hollowed out and turned into artistic bowls.

Woody plants: Woody plants have hard stems and buds, which survive, above ground in winter. For example, trees are woody plants. 'Herbaceous plants' are the opposite of 'woody plants'.

Index